FORGOTTEN RAIDERS OF '42

POTOMAC'S MILITARY CONTROVERSIES

Gettysburg: The Meade-Sickles Controversy
by Richard A. Sauers

*"Friends in Peace and War": The Russian Navy's
Landmark Visit to Civil War San Francisco*
by C. Douglas Kroll

The Pearl Harbor Myth: Rethinking the Unthinkable
by George Victor

FORGOTTEN RAIDERS OF '42

THE FATE OF THE MARINES LEFT BEHIND ON MAKIN

Tripp Wiles

POTOMAC BOOKS, INC.
WASHINGTON, D.C.

Copyright © 2007 Tripp Wiles

Library of Congress Cataloging-in-Publication Data
Wiles, Tripp.
  Forgotten raiders of '42 : the fate of the Marines left behind on Makin / Tripp Wiles.—1st ed.
    p. cm. — (Potomac's military controversies series)
  Includes bibliographical references and index.
  ISBN-13: 978-1-59797-055-6 (alk. paper)
  ISBN-10: 1-59797-055-7 (alk. paper)
  1. Makin Atoll, Raid on, Kiribati, 1942. 2. United States. Marine Corps. Marine Raider Battalion, 2nd. 3. World War, 1939–1945—Prisoners and prisoners, Japanese. 4. World War, 1939–1945—Amphibious operations. 5. World War, 1939–1945—Atrocities—Kiribati—Makin Atoll. 6. Prisoners of war—United States—Death. 7. Prisoners of war—Kiribati—Makin Atoll—Death. I. Title.
  D767.917.W47 2007
  940.54'26681—dc22

                                                          2006031930

Printed in the United States of America on acid-free paper that meets the American National Standards Institute Z39-48 Standard.

Potomac Books, Inc.
22841 Quicksilver Drive
Dulles, Virginia 20166

First Edition

10 9 8 7 6 5 4 3 2 1

THANKS TO RAIDER VETERAN BEN CARSON.
HIS UNWAVERING COMMITMENT TO THE MEMORY AND HONOR
OF THE FALLEN RAIDERS IS THE REASON THIS STORY WAS TOLD.

TO MY WIFE, LINDSAY, FOR HER AMAZING LOVE AND SUPPORT.

CONTENTS

PREFACE

On October 16, 1942, on the fringe of the Japanese Empire, members of the Imperial Japanese Navy's Sixth Base Unit ceremoniously beheaded nine American men of the Second Marine Raider Battalion on Kwajalein Island. These men had no hope for a pardon or a last-minute commando rescue as they walked one by one, blindfolded, to their execution spot and what would become their burial site. The Raiders' families and their commander thought they were already dead, and the men knew this.

These volunteer patriots, unbeknownst to their command, had been inadvertently left behind after the Makin Island raid of August 1942. The raid, which was a morale boost for the Navy and the American public, was hailed at home as a tactical and strategic success even as the condemned Raiders knelt to await their fate. The details of the raid's shaky beginning and tragic end, however, would not be made known until years later.

CHRONOLOGY

August 17 and 18, 1942	Second U.S. Marine Raider Battalion raids Makin Island.
August 30, 1942	The Japanese take nine Raiders to Kwajalein Island.
September 2, 1942	Nine Raiders arrive on Kwajalein.
October 16, 1942	The Japanese execute nine Raiders on Kwajalein.
July 1943	Capt. Louis Silvie Zamperini arrives on Kwajalein and sees the Raiders' names on a prison wall.
November 21, 1943	The United States invades and captures Makin.
February 1944	The United States invades and captures Kwajalein.

November 1945	War crimes trials are conducted on Kwajalein.
May 1946	Koso Abe is tried on war crimes charges in Guam.
June 1947	Koso Abe is hanged after being convicted on war crimes charges.
November 1999	The United States recovers the Raiders' remains from Makin Island.
January 2002	The United States attempts to recover the nine executed Raiders' remains from Kwajalein.
May 2002	A plaque dedicated to the "mistakenly left behind" Raiders is erected on Kwajalein.
November 2003	A new plaque, without the words "left behind," is erected on Kwajalein.

INTRODUCTION

The Second Marine Raider Battalion's commando raid on Makin Island in August 1942 was an audacious move in the early stages of America's war in the Pacific. The raid brought hope to the American people and destruction to the Japanese forces on Makin. Unfortunately, nine Marine Raiders were left on Makin after the raid and were unable to witness the homecoming or accolades that followed the invasion. Because it was not known until much later that the nine Raiders had been left behind and because they were executed, the story and circumstances of their captivity and death have not yet been extensively covered. And although the left-behind Raiders' demise has been relegated to only a few sentences in most histories of the raid, their fellow Raiders have not forgotten them.

The Makin raid has been deemed "the most spectacular commando operation of the Pacific war."[1] Wartime monographs, popular media, and even some recent histories have portrayed the raid as a success that experienced few difficulties. Despite veterans' revelations of the raid's troubles in the years since

World War II, a close examination of the situation that resulted in the abandonment of nine men has not been forthcoming. The Navy's immediate knowledge of the near disasters of the Makin raid has not been discussed. Perhaps more important, however, the nine Raiders' full story, from the time they were declared missing until their execution, has not been told. Japanese war criminals' self-serving testimony has until recently been the sole source of the left-behind Raiders' story.

The media has documented the courage and will displayed by the Raider force on Makin. Unfortunately, the decisions of the Raider commander that led to several mishaps have been left out of the media's accounts. While we may understand why the full story of the mission was not presented during the war, the truth about the nine Raiders' abandonment is now long overdue.

The purpose of this book is to tell the nine Raiders' story, to go beyond the summaries of the circumstances of their abandonment, captivity, and execution given in past histories of the raid. In presenting what for years has been avoided, the author hopes that the facts of the raid's mishaps and consequences will answer the question, Why were these men left behind?

While this book intends to record the story of the nine left-behind Marine Raiders, it also examines how such a tragedy occurred during a raid that was hailed by the Navy and historians as a success. Until now no one has presented the full extent of the Navy's knowledge concerning the breakdown of command during the raid or how that breakdown was linked to the Raiders' abandonment. Using old records as well as new evidence, this study details the circumstances that led to the raid commander's neglect of his men.

Information about the weeks the nine Raiders spent in captivity has been limited, while the successes of the raid— real and exaggerated—have been well publicized. The nine

Raiders' story is directly linked to decisions made during the raid that were known by the Navy at the time. The evidence herein provides the Navy's true assessment of the raid. The following work deals with the events that led to the Raiders' abandonment and capture as well. Details of the Raiders' captivity have traditionally been pulled from Japanese war criminals' testimonies, but herein the author examines additional sources that tell a much different version of the conditions that the Raiders lived and died under on the island.

Historians have written about the Second Marine Raider Battalion's August 1942 raid on Japanese-held Makin Island since shortly after the Raiders' return. The raid marked the first time in U.S. naval history that an assault was launched from submarines. In the daring raid, the United States took its fight to an island held by the Japanese Empire and destroyed its enemy. At the war's end, revelations of the Raiders' troubles on the island came to light, and as the years went by, veterans' accounts of the raid continued to provide new insight.

Following the Navy's lead, the early historical monographs and Pacific theater histories lauded the raid as a strategic success and a psychological victory for the American people. Good news and heroes were what those at home needed in the summer of 1942, and they were given them via the Navy Cross–awarded raid commander, Lt. Col. Evans F. Carlson, and his daring "gung ho" Marine Raiders. Freshly published accounts, and later a movie, of the raid helped the Navy capitalize on the morale boost that the strike into enemy territory had produced.[2]

Since the war, however, historians have expressed differing opinions on the raid's success and its effects on U.S. war strategy in the Pacific. Lieutenant Colonel Carlson's leadership in the raid has also been questioned since it was learned in 1946 that nine Marine Raiders were left behind alive on Makin. News that the Japanese had beheaded these nine men, as well as veterans' accounts of the harried withdrawal from the island and the Raiders' attempted surrender to their enemy, presented a completely different story than the one depicted by the Navy early on.

It may seem as though the raid's mishaps and the raid commander's ill-fated decisions were late revelations. The after-action reports make it clear, however, that privately the Navy knew that some of the bravest men in Marine Corps history had been let down and that the Navy had barely escaped a complete disaster. Lieutenant Colonel Carlson's after-action report, the written comments of submarine commanders and Pacific Fleet commander Adm. Chester W. Nimitz, as well as Raider veterans' memoirs and statements detail the unfortunate and avoidable command and control breakdown that marred the raid.

While recent historians have described the situation that directly led to the Raiders' abandonment, the actions on the first night of the raid have not been linked to the tragedy. Futhermore, what happened to the nine Raiders between their abandonment on Makin and their deaths on Kwajalein Island has never been examined or accurately detailed. The unpublished memoirs, Navy investigation reports, interviews, and trial proceedings from the Navy war crimes trial of Vice Adm. Koso Abe in 1946 reveal the circumstances of the Raiders' fate as well as the justice that was served to the Japanese war criminals.

Though war-era historians were not privy to all of the facts of the raid that are available today, postwar historians did have access to the new details. Amazingly some Makin raid histories gloss over the lapses in leadership and some fail to mention the Raiders' execution. One of these postwar histories seems to be a continuation of the Navy's whitewashed account of the raid. Theodore Roscoe's *United States Submarine Operations in World War II* was written for the Bureau of Naval Personnel.[3]

The foreword is written by Admiral Nimitz, whose after-action report on the raid describes a much different action than the one described in Roscoe's book.

United States Submarine Operations in World War II, as the title suggests, focuses on the submarine aspect of the Makin raid. Although it was first printed in 1949, five years after the discovery of the Raiders' execution, Roscoe makes no mention of the men left behind. Roscoe also calls the raid the greatest in the Pacific theater in World War II, a brilliant exploit in Lieutenant Colonel Carlson's career, and a highly successful mission. In describing the Raiders' return, he writes the submarines set the course "when the last man was aboard."[4]

Battle Submerged: Submarine Fighters of World War II by Rear Adm. Harley Cope and Capt. Walter Karig includes a chapter about the raid that, like Roscoe's book, focuses on the submarine effort.[5] *Battle Submerged*, published in 1951, also fails to mention the executed Raiders. Instead, the authors describe Makin installations burning in the wake of the Pearl Harbor–bound submarines.[6]

Samuel Elliot Morison, author of *History of the United States Naval Operations in World War II*, volume 4, *Coral Sea, Midway and Submarine Actions, May 1942–August 1942*, aptly calls the Makin raid the "most ambitious" of submarine special missions.[7] Morison's description of the raid's failures and its tragic ending, though, are in sharp contrast to his counterparts' writings at the time. Although Morison's book was published in 1949, he managed to devote much attention to the missing Raiders and their fate. He even touches on the controversial issue of the command-endorsed surrender note to the Japanese.

Most recent histories often include accounts of the Raiders' chaotic withdrawal to the submarines and of the nine stranded Marines. Maj. Gen. Oscar F. Peatross, USMC (ret.), who was a lieutenant on the Makin Island raid, devoted a chapter to the mission in his book *Bless 'Em All: The Marine Raiders of World War II*.[8] This chapter provides the most comprehensive published look at the abandoned Raiders. His retelling of the raid also calls into question Lieutenant Colonel Carlson's decisions and their consequences, which included the Raiders' return to Hawaii without nine men. Because General Peatross's platoon was separated from the rest of the battalion throughout the raid, his book presents a unique view of the battle as well as interviews of Raiders conducted shortly after the raid.

General Peatross's account is much different than that of his fellow Raider, Lt. W. S. LeFrançois, who in 1943 provided one of the first published accounts of the raid in the *Saturday Evening Post* article "We Mopped Up Makin."[9] Lieutenant LeFrançois gave the public insight into the difficulties of the raid and the overwhelming obstacles he and the other Raiders overcame in order to return alive. LeFrançois's account, written before the Raiders' execution was revealed, does not describe the failure of command and control on the night of August 17. As such, his version was the perfect script for the Raider war film *Gung Ho*.[10]

Playwright Michael Blankfort wrote *The Big Yankee*, the biography of Lieutenant Colonel Carlson.[11] The quotes and description of Carlson in this book read like a screenplay. To his credit, Blankfort's notes mention the executed Raiders and Carlson's statement about the incident. He does not, however, provide an objective look at the Makin raid or its commander.

The most inaccurate and least detailed histories of the Makin raid have presented, at worst, something that did not happen and, at best, a tribute to the Raiders' actions. Some histories of the raid have portrayed the Raiders' unbelievable courage as well as the unfortunate hasty withdrawal and the nine Raiders' abandonment. No history, though, has described the stranded Raiders' last days and examined in detail what caused them to be left behind.

The nine abandoned Marines were captives of the Japanese Empire's unyielding concepts of "honor." Their stories are directly linked to the similar fate that met several other American patriots who followed them. Although the Raiders were the only Americans to be executed on Kwajalein in the fall of 1942, they were not the only Americans to die there during the war. Army bomber crews and other American fliers were imprisoned and executed on Kwajalein.[12] The investigations into their deaths by the Navy war crimes investigators provide some sense of what life on the island may have been like for the Raiders. Like the Raiders' story, the stories of these men have been largely untold as well. This book also incorporates the related stories of other Kwajalein prisoners of war (POWs), whose last days also have been forgotten.

Fortunately not all the Americans who were imprisoned on Kwajalein were executed. In fact, a few men lived to tell their stories. Their stories are not only similar to but are directly related to the stories of the Makin Raiders. Their testimony provides evidence that contradicts what most people believe concerning the Raiders' captivity.

What happened to the Raiders from the time of the raid until their deaths has been inadequately addressed by historians. Who were these men? How could a raid that went so "well" have resulted in men left behind alive? Who was responsible for the abandoned Raiders' situation? How were the Raiders captured? How were they treated? What did their interrogation consist of? Why were they executed? How were they executed? Where were they executed and buried? This work provides insight into the circumstances of the Raiders' abandonment and the conditions under which they lived and died.

Those who knew better unfortunately encouraged historical distortion of the Makin raid. By going back to the original surveyors of the raid's results, very different conclusions can be made about the raid than those that were made in historical monographs of the time. A more accurate account can be presented of the preparation for the raid, the raid's events, the casualties on both sides, and the raid's aftermath.

This story is limited because its subjects were killed many years ago. Also, the state of war that existed between the United States and Japan and the confined nature of other Americans' time spent on Kwajalein during the war limits the knowledge of the layout and environment on the island. To compound these difficulties, several of the men involved in investigating this crime are no longer living. Fading memories and memories not written down have further hampered the telling of this story.

While U.S. naval investigators, Japanese language officers, and Judge Adjutant General (JAG) officers associated with the 1946–48 war crimes trial conducted in Guam are living, the two men who were close to this case, U.S. naval investigation veterans David Osborne and William P. Mahoney, recently died. Osborne and Mahoney talked with witnesses of the Raiders' capture, imprisonment, and execution. They also interrogated the men who beheaded the Raiders. While much of their investigation has been written down, these men may not have recorded everything they discovered during their interviews and interrogations.

This study begins with a summary of the Makin Island raid. Particular attention is paid to the Raiders' withdrawal from the island and the decisions of Lieutenant Colonel Carlson that directly affected the men who were left behind. The actions, inactions, and conditions that led to the unintentional abandonment of the nine Raiders are examined as well. Previous histories, after-action reports, and accounts by other Raiders provide the basis for this summary.

In this book, conclusions are drawn as to who these nine men were and how they came to be left behind. The men's actions are documented to record the selfless service they exhibited. An unpublished eyewitness report from a Makin Island native is used to lend insight into the Raiders' condition and actions shortly after their abandonment. This document along with Japanese histories is used to illustrate the threat the Raiders faced upon their departure and what should have happened concerning a full accounting of Raiders before they left the island.

The next phase of the book outlines and examines the after-action reports made by the Navy command of the mission. The reports of the task group commander, Cdr. John Haines, and the Pacific Fleet commander, Adm. Chester Nimitz, are used to present the Navy's private appraisal of the raid. Because the evaluation reports offer only subdued criticism, the officers' tone and word selection are also highlighted.

Finally, the experiences on Kwajalein of surviving American prisoners of war and how they relate to the nine Raiders are examined. Interviews of these former POWs are used to depict the conditions the Raiders faced. Recent interviews of Marshallese witnesses to the Raiders' imprisonment are presented as well. The unpublished memoirs of a Navy war crimes investigator provide new details of the Raiders' capture by the Japanese. These memoirs describe the prisoners' captors and executioners. Additional information is collected from the war crimes testimony and personal memoirs of the men charged with the nine Marine Raiders' execution. A further goal of this book is to complete the picture of the last days of the nine Marine Raiders and illuminate the courage they exhibited. The men of the Second Marine Raider Battalion had volunteered to fight and participate in high-risk missions. Historians cannot say enough about the courage these men displayed, and the sacrifices they were willing to and did make. As a former Raider put it, "We were there!" and "When the job was to be done, it was completed."[13] Because of the Makin raid survivors' fortitude and the sacrifices of fellow Raiders who did not return, the mishaps of the raid and the failures of the Raiders' leadership should not be ignored.

This book aims to fully document the Raiders' disappearance and execution and to record their story. A full discussion about the Makin raid and the executed men, who have until now been footnotes in history, is presented in this book. A variety of sources make the case that the raid's success was not as it has been portrayed, and the realities of the raid are the reason for the nightmare that followed. These sources have been brought together to better record the story and the circumstances of nine brave Americans who where accidentally left behind alive by their unit, executed by their enemy, and forgotten by history.

Chapter One

THE RAIDERS

Early on the morning of August 17, 1942, the USS *Argonaut* and the USS *Nautilus* opened their hatches and released A and B companies of the Second Marine Raider Battalion into less than favorable conditions. The 222 Raiders, in rafts equipped with unreliable outboard motors, slipped away from the submarines into the choppy Pacific waters of the Gilbert Islands and into history.[1] Their mission was to raid Japanese-held Makin and Little Makin islands in the hopes of diverting enemy forces from Guadalcanal.[2] In addition to hitting the enemy on his own soil and diverting forces, the U.S. Navy hoped the mission would boost the nation's morale by providing Americans with tangible evidence, via news reports, that their military was striking back.

The Second Marine Raiders were the first men in U.S. history to conduct an amphibious raid from a submarine. But the material for war reporters, Hollywood, military historians, and novelists did not end there.[3] In fact, the events of the two-day raid and the Raiders' actions made the Makin raid and the Raiders famous for years to come.

Like the raid itself, the Raider commander, World War I Army veteran Lt Col. Evans F. Carlson, was neither conventional nor traditional. As a Marine observer, Carlson had encountered guerrilla warfare in Nicaragua and spent life-changing years in China with Communist forces. Branded "red" by many of his counterparts, Carlson's career assignments were very different from most Marine Corps officers'.[4] Lieutenant Colonel Carlson's time in China made such an impression on him that he wrote books about Chinese Communism and resigned from the military to speak against the Japanese enemy after being muzzled by the corps.[5] The Chinese Communists' fighting philosophy also greatly affected Carlson's outlook on U.S. military tactics. As a result of his time spent with the Chinese, Carlson's views on unit cohesion, military discipline, hierarchy, and war-fighting skills were dramatically contrary to those of the Marine Corps. While he might not have been the embodiment of Marine Corps molding, his courage and enthusiasm were undeniable among his peers. Even Carlson's strongest critics thought his courage under fire was beyond question.[6]

The Second Marine Raider Battalion's executive officer was Maj. James Roosevelt, President Franklin Roosevelt's son. Carlson had known Major Roosevelt since he, as a member of the presidential guard detachment in Warm Springs, Georgia, became acquainted with FDR and the president's family at the presidential retreat in 1935.[7] In fact, Carlson was on a familiar enough basis with the president that later, while he was assigned to China, he sent secret updates to FDR, addressing the letters to the president's secretary, Marguerite LeHand.[8] In addition to being a friend of the Roosevelts', Carlson had worked with the president's wife, Eleanor, in attempts to convince Congress to send money to Chinese cooperatives.[9] Carlson had allies among the Roosevelt family and the much needed political sway for a man of his convictions.

Carlson's strong belief that the U.S. military should adopt Chinese Communist guerrilla tactics had an influence on the president's son. As a result, Major Roosevelt was an early advocate of the Raider battalions. In January 1942 he wrote to Marine Corps commandant Maj. Gen. Thomas Holcomb and requested a commando unit be created with "purposes similar to the British Commandos and the Chinese Guerrillas."[10]

Roosevelt was preceded in calling for the commando unit by the president's senior intelligence adviser and the eventual father of the Office of Strategic Services (OSS), William J. Donovan. Donovan, a World War I Army hero, had made a proposal for a guerrilla unit to FDR a month before James, and Donovan requested that he be allowed to form the new unit.[11]

In June 1941 Gen. Holland Smith, who was tasked with implementing the Marine Corps' 1935 amphibious warfare doctrine before the United States entered World War II[12] and who in 1941 commanded the Amphibious Force Atlantic Fleet, appointed Lt. Col. Meritt A. Edson to command the First Battalion Fifth Marines. Acting on his designs to transform the Marine Corps' amphibious operations, General Smith designated the battalion to serve permanently with a naval APD squadron. Smith considered APDs, which were destroyer transports, the best transportation available for an amphibious Marine strike force.[13] Smith wanted to separate this newly formed unit from the rest of the division when he formed it, but a lack of manpower prevented him from doing so. By January 1942, however, manpower was no longer a problem because the United States had entered World War II, and Smith requested that General Holcomb designate the battalion. The request was granted, and the First Separate Battalion was formed one week prior to Roosevelt's letter requesting the formation of Raider battalions.

On February 4, 1942, the Second Separate Battalion was

created, and the Second Marine Division commander placed Carlson in charge of it with Roosevelt as his executive officer. Later that same month the First and Second Separate battalions became the Marine Raider battalions.[14]

Although the Raider concept and Carlson's leadership were endorsed by Roosevelt, many in the Navy and Marine Corps did not share the president's enthusiasm for the Raider battalions. Both the Raiders and Lieutenant Colonel Carlson were met with great skepticism that continued long after the Makin raid and until the Raider battalions' disbandment. Maj. James Roosevelt noted, "There was considerable jealousy on the part of Marine Corps officers because of [Carlson's] ability (I think frankly sometimes through the President's intervention) to get different ideas and better equipment for his men from the naval establishments."[15]

Adding to fellow officers' jealousy was Carlson's refusal to follow the Marine Corps' designs for the Raider battalions. General Holcomb had ordered one-third of Edson's men to be transferred from First Battalion Headquarters in Quantico, Virginia, to the Second Marine Raider Battalion in San Diego, California. Carlson rejected half of Edson's men.[16] Instead, he personally interviewed Raider candidates and handpicked his men from volunteers. First and foremost, his men had to be eager to fight the Japanese, and they had to know what they were fighting for.[17]

Carlson felt that because of its uniqueness the specialty command he was given was the perfect means by which he could apply the techniques he had learned abroad. Lieutenant Colonel Carlson made the Raiders' training isolated and self-contained at Camp Elliot on Jacques Farms in the hills outside San Diego, California.[18] The atmosphere he created at the camp was hermetic even for the Marine Corps.

As commander of the Raiders, the assiduous Carlson

wasted no time implementing the ethics he had observed during his time with the Communist Chinese. The Raiders' slogan became the Chinese term *gung ho,* meaning "work together." The Marine Corps' traditionally strict chain of command became blurred among the Raiders and in many cases nonexistent under Carlson's command.

Carlson's application of Chinese guerrilla methodology inspired some of his Marines. One of Carlson's radiomen, Raider K. L. McCullough, remembers the colonel as being the most dedicated American he had ever met.[19] Other "Old Corps" Marines such as 2nd Lt. Charles Lamb, a former sergeant major, did not embrace Carlson's new approach to leadership and considered it to be "double talk and ridicule of the Marine Corps."[20] Even many of the young Raiders were suspicious of their "ethical indoctrination" at Camp Elliot, which was contrary to their limited experiences in boot camp.[21]

While Carlson believed it was his privilege to lead, he did not believe a leader should have special privileges. Carlson's leadership and unit cohesion philosophies were different from anything the Marines had ever seen before. According to James Roosevelt, "All of the officers had to participate exactly as the men."[22] Carlson rid his camp of traditional officers' and noncommissioned officers' (NCOs) messes, so the Raiders could eat together. Carlson took the suggestions and thoughts of men of all ranks, and his Raiders were allowed to air their opinions as well as their grievances in gung ho meetings.[23] Carlson stressed "decentralized decision making."[24] His style of leadership and the atmosphere it created greatly affected the events of the Makin raid.

Carlson's unorthodox philosophical training was coupled with intense physical fitness and weapons training. According to Raider Denton E. Hudman, forty-mile hikes were common. Raider Ben Carson recalls Carlson's development of a fire team centered on an M-1 rifleman, a Browning automatic rifleman, and a Thompson submachine gunner.[25] In addition to their training at Camp Elliot, the Raiders trained on three APDs off the southern California coast and practiced assaults on San Clemente Island.[26]

"The training was rigid," remembers Kenneth H. "Mudhole" Merrill. "It was full of force marches and knife throwing." Merrill, a private in the weapons platoon, received his nickname from Maj. James Roosevelt while training on Jacques Farms. One time, Merrill did not have any water left in his canteen, so he got down on the ground and started drinking out of a mud hole. Roosevelt noticed this and yelled, "Hey Mud Hole!" The name stuck.

Roosevelt was also the man who interviewed Merrill for the Raiders. Merrill was sixteen at the time so he had to lie about his age to be admitted in the battalion. Merrill recalled that Roosevelt did everything he could to help the Raiders and their training. According to Merrill, "If we needed something like Thompson machine guns, he'd disappear for about twenty-four hours and call the old man. Before you knew it we'd have what we needed."[27]

With the Raiders' initial training in California complete, the battalion boarded the USS *Franklin Bell* (APA-16) in San Diego and set sail for Hawaii. There they would train under the eyes of the Pacific Fleet and Pacific Ocean areas commander in chief, Adm. Chester Nimitz. The ship arrived in the still-decimated Pearl Harbor on May 18, 1942.[28] Training was put on hold, however, when Nimitz ordered the C and D companies to protect island garrisons at Midway.[29]

Charlie Company was tasked with beach defense of Sand Island while D Company fortified Eastern Island. The Japanese attack was turned back in the fateful Midway victory, and the Raiders, though attacked from the air, were not harmed. With Midway secure, the Raiders returned to Oahu.[30]

On Oahu, at Camp Catlin and Barbers Point, the battalion prepared for its mission to Makin. The Raiders coordinated with the Navy in preparation for a raid on Oahu as well. The Makin mission was organized under a task group led by Cdr. John Haines. Lieutenant Colonel Carlson was made commander of the task force that included the Raider battalion.

Commander Haines requested that the task group be given three submarines, one of which would be used as the command post. This request was denied, and instead the submarines USS *Argonaut* and USS *Nautilus* were chosen to transport the task group to Makin.[31] Commander Haines made his command post the USS *Nautilus*, which was commanded by Lt. Cdr. W. H. Brockman. Lt. Cdr. J. R. Pierce, who five months after the Makin raid went down with his ship off of New Britain, commanded the USS *Argonaut*.[32] The two submarines left Pearl Harbor on August 8, 1942, and the sub commanders transported the Raider force to their destination without incident or detection.

Chapter Two

THE RAID

The raid, on Makin Island began much like it ended—not as planned. On August 17 at 0330 hours, after having traveled for ten days from Hawaii in cramped and hot submarines, the Raiders left the dark vessels for the darker waters. The disembarkation from the submarines into rafts equipped with faulty outboard engines made for an awkward start. The impossible task of rendezvousing the twenty boats before heading for the beach immediately created an unmanageable mess on the water.

Matters were further complicated by a change in plans. After assessing the swift current, the strong wind conditions, the heavy swells, and the nonfunctioning Evinrude outboard motors, Carlson decided that both companies should hit the beach together. The colonel felt that the landing had to be accomplished before daylight and that the confusion in the water made changing the landing plans imperative.[1] Not all of the Raiders heard that their orders had changed, and unfortunately this was the first of many breakdowns in communication during the raid.

One of the men who did not get the word was Lt. Oscar F. Peatross. Peatross took Lieutenant Colonel Carlson to the rendezvous point and then dropped him off in another raft, into what he recalls was mass confusion.[2] Because they didn't receive the change in orders, Lieutenant Peatross and his men landed half a mile to the southwest of the rest of the battalion.

As Carlson and the Raiders hit the beach, the already mixed A and B companies became badly intermingled.[3] Within a few minutes of landing, an overanxious Marine accidentally discharged his weapon, ruining the battalion's chance for a surprise attack. Lieutenant Colonel Carlson's frustrations began to mount with his troops' confusion, and this frustration was evident in the colonel's first radio transmission to the *Nautilus*: "Everything lousy."[4]

While the bulk of the Raider battalion regrouped on the island's periphery, Carlson sent part of A Company across the island toward the lagoon. B Company was ordered to wait in reserve and provide security for A Company's left flank. The Raiders' desire to seek out the enemy was high and some began self-initiated scouting forays to hunt for the Japanese. A Company's first objective was to clear the Government House, a hut near the beach once used by the British, which, to the Raiders' surprise, was uninhabited. To their further surprise, another Raider element had also made it to the Government House. The confusion of commingled companies combined with an early lack of command and control and amended orders made for a dangerous mix.

As the Raiders pushed forward, the island natives awoke. The natives were friendly and willing to help and supplied the Raiders' with an estimate of the number of Japanese on the island. Unfortunately this estimate was greater than the enemy's actual troop strength, but Carlson, erring on the side of caution, took it to heart. The colonel's initial cautiousness hindered his decision making and the Raider's progress throughout the raid.

An hour after landing and shortly after daybreak, the southwest-bound Raider element, comprised primarily of A Company, met the enemy on the road outside of his defensive position. The Japanese had rushed along the road toward the Government House on bicycles and a truck after being alerted to the Americans' arrival.

The fighting was close and soon became fierce, with automatic weapons fire and little cover. A number of brave Raiders as well as desperate Japanese defenders lost their lives. Sgt. Clyde Thomason died early in the battle while directing fire. Thomason was awarded the Medal of Honor posthumously for his bravery and was the first enlisted Marine to be awarded the medal in World War II.[5]

Well-placed snipers and enemy machine-gun positions hampered the Raider force. The expertly camouflaged snipers fired from coconut trees and accounted for the majority of Raider losses.[6] Raider veterans recall a close pitched battle and the necessity to constantly search for cover among the taro patches, breadfruit, and coconut trees.[7] Although the Japanese defenders were able to slow the Raiders' progress, their time was running out, and they knew it. "We are all dying in battle" was the last message sent out by Japanese sergeant major Kanemitsu.[8]

The diary of Adm. Matome Ogaki notes the Japanese's accurate appraisal of their situation on Makin at the time. Ogaki also seems to suggest that, although the Sixth Naval Base force commander, Vice Adm. Koso Abe, responded with reinforcements, the Japanese were not fooled by U.S. attempts to divert forces from Guadalcanal: "About two hundred enemy Marines landed on Makin in the Gilberts from two submarines after 0300, and our garrison is fighting hard. The commander, Sixth Naval Base Force, ordered a rescue attack, but it is doubtful whether they can hold out. . . . Anyway such an enemy trick will be nothing to us."[9]

Meanwhile Peatross and his men, who had been unable to find the Raider party upon landing, moved toward the original linkup point. Peatross's radio did not work, and he was still unaware of Carlson's change in plans. Thus, he continued to follow the original plan: "The scheme of maneuver called for us to land under the cover of darkness on the weather side of Butaritari [the native name for Makin] with Company 'A' on the left opposite on Chong's Wharf (Beach 'Y') and Company 'B' on the right opposite Government Wharf (Beach 'Z'). Each company was then to cross the island, turn ('A' to the right and 'B' to the left), and advance toward the center of the objective area, meeting in the vicinity of the church."[10]

Upon reaching the preestablished rendezvous at the island's church, Peatross and his men heard a firefight erupt. Peatross moved his men to the road, where they were able to kill three bicycle-riding Japanese defenders. Although they did not recognize him at the time, they also killed the commander of the one-hundred-man garrison, Sergeant Major Kanemitsu, near the Japanese headquarters.[11] Three of Peatross's men were killed as they attempted to knock out a machine gunner.[12]

At around 0700 hours Peatross heard the *Nautilus* fire its deck guns. The submarine was raining salvos on the Japanese position in response to a call from A Company for fire. The submarine fire on the raid was excellent—in terms of both accuracy and effectiveness—considering that poor radio communications meant the subs did not have spotters calling to correct the fire on the island. Shortly after firing on the enemy positions, *Nautilus* commander William H. Brockman redirected fire and sunk two enemy ships entering the lagoon from the west.[13]

Peatross soon realized that "all of the Japanese" were between him and Carlson's main body. To confirm his belief, the lieutenant sent Cpl. Sam Brown, Pvt. Alexander J. Donovan, and Pvt. Raymond D. Jansen to reconnoiter the island's south-west end. The small patrol returned with confirmation that the area was clear. Peatross knew it was important to get this information to Lieutenant Colonel Carlson, but before he could do so a group of seventy-five natives approached Peatross and his men coming from the battle area. Speaking limited English, the group further confirmed the enemy's location. Peatross immediately sent out Privates Donovan and Jansen to relay the information to Carlson. Although enemy fire forced Jansen to return to Peatross, Donovan made it through to Carlson.[14]

Poor positions and hidden sniper fire had debilitated the Raiders' force, and their situation was stagnant for the next four hours. According to Carlson, the pattern of the enemy had been clear since 0700: "four machine guns, two grenade throwers, automatic rifles, and a flame thrower, with infantry supporting the automatic weapons and with a corps of snipers operating from the tops of coconut trees."[15] Raider Kenneth Merrill recalls knocking out one especially tough machine gunners' nest: "At about 10:30 a.m. we ran into this Japanese machine-gun nest that was holding everybody up. Me and Chapman couldn't understand it. Every time we'd kill the gunner the gun would keep blasting. Fortunately they weren't adjusting their fire so they were shooting over our heads. When they finally did stop the firing we saw there were eighteen of them in there. So every time we killed a gunner another one had been taking his place. When I saw all eighteen of them in there I damn near threw up. [A Raider] threw a grenade in there just to make sure they were all dead. It was a mess."[16]

At 1130 hours two enemy reconnaissance planes flew along the island for several minutes and then dropped two wayward bombs. The bombs were immediately followed by what would become typical of Japanese defenders in the Pacific: a Banzai attack. According to Raider lieutenant W. S. LeFrançois, the Japanese, signaled by a bugler, ran along the road at full stride with their fixed bayonets overhead and firing and shouting, "Banzai!"[17] The futile charge was easily repelled and was disastrous for the enemy.

Two hours later a mixed force of twelve Japanese reconnaissance bombers, Zero fighters, seaplanes, and armed Kawanishi flying boats flew over Makin. Concentrating their fire along the road, the enemy bombed and strafed the island for over an hour to no avail. One of the Kawanishi flying boats and a reconnaissance bomber landed in the lagoon and were immediately engaged by Raider machine-gun and Boys anti-tank rifle fire. The reconnaissance plane was hit and burned. The flying boat, also hit by Raider fire, took off from the water and then crashed into the lagoon.

Shortly afterward, First Lieutenant Peatross's messenger, Private Donovan, arrived at the Raider main body to report the favorable enemy situation to the southwest. Although Carlson later told Peatross that Donovan's news was the "high point" of the first day, it was clear to Peatross that Carlson did not act on the information. Peatross felt that Carlson had "convinced himself that that the enemy was strong and, having done so, subconsciously rejected all facts to the contrary." Peatross was amazed that Carlson did not make use of the intelligence: "He seems to have discounted or completely ignored Donovan's information on the enemy situation. Instead he chose to remain in a defensive posture and made no attempt to link up with my group, thereby leaving the initiative in the hands of a few snipers."[18]

Despite the fresh intelligence and the Raiders' destruction of the Japanese planes and all enemy troops aboard, Lieutenant Colonel Carlson again erred on the side of caution. He took to heart false reports from the natives that thirty-five enemy reinforcements had offloaded from the Kawanishi flight and that more were expected to arrive.[19] Having been bogged down for several hours and with snipers slowly chipping away at his forces, Carlson decided to pull back. The Japanese quickly moved forward onto the ground the Raiders had abandoned, and at 1630, as enemy aircraft again bombed the island, the enemy on the ground were subjected to the ordnance that had been intended for the Raiders.

Lieutenant Colonel Carlson's men, the USS *Nautilus*'s fire, and even the enemy's own bombs had left an already small force of Japanese defenders decimated. Only a few of the enemy remained alive. However, because of their bold ground attacks, unconfirmed intelligence, and three enemy air attacks, Lieutenant Colonel Carlson felt it was time to go. The Raiders had not finished destroying the enemy forces and installations, yet Carlson chose to call for a return to the submarines, citing the "time agreed on for withdrawal was 1930" and the enemy's apparent strength.[20]

Shortly before 1900 hours the Raiders withdrew to the beach. The Raiders' preparation for return to the submarines began as planned. Carlson established a covering force on the beach, and the first boats hit the water at 1915. According to Lieutenant Colonel Carlson, he and the covering force left the beach at 1930 and headed toward the submarines.

Lieutenant Colonel Carlson called what happened next a "ghastly nightmare."[21] It could also be called a withdrawal disaster. The hard-hitting surf capsized Raider rafts and drowned out the coil and magneto-exposed motors, just as it had on the way in to Makin.[22] The surf formed an impenetrable wall between the Raiders and the submarines. The Raiders' equipment and many weapons were dumped into the sea, and the men were thrown back on the beach. The Raiders tried desperately to break through for hours, but the waves and current were unrelenting. The insurmountable water obstacle left many of the Raiders spent and without protection.

Meanwhile, Lieutenant Peatross and his men, having received no word from Carlson, began to wonder what was going on. According to Peatross, it seemed as though the main body had missed an excellent chance to link up with them. Peatross decided to wait a while longer. He and his men went back to the headquarters building, destroyed the radio, and took a few souvenirs.[23]

As the sun began to set Peatross realized that Carlson did not plan to link up with him and his men. The men moved back across the island. They inflated their boat and filled up the engine with gasoline. Because the surf was high, Peatross watched the rhythm of the waves for about fifteen minutes. At approximately 1930 Peatross's party put the raft into the water and paddled until the motor was started. Fifteen minutes later the men saw the green light of the *Nautilus* and headed for the sub. Peatross learned upon boarding the USS *Nautilus* that he and his men were the only ones to have made it back. Visions of a prolonged battle on Makin and comrades stranded on the island led Peatross to request permission to return.[24]

On Makin, unarmed, half-naked, drenched Raiders washed back onto the beach exhausted. Some continued to try to swim through the surf while others found shelter and tried to rest.[25] The condition of Lieutenant Colonel Carlson's unit had changed drastically. Carlson later said that the situation was extremely grave and that his force had been stripped of its fighting power. The impossible conditions combined with his sudden loss of command and control caused Carlson great concern and led to what he recalled as "the spiritual low point" of the mission.[26] Without a means to leave the island, the Raiders became desperate.

One Raider, Pvt. Howard R. Craven, borrowed Major

Roosevelt's flashlight and signaled the submarines for assistance. The *Argonaut* replied that it would pick up the Raiders at the lagoon at 0300. The senior Marine onboard the submarine, Lieutenant Plunley, advised the commander to postpone the rendezvous, and the rescue attempt was eventually cancelled. When the submarines failed to show, Craven, Cpl. Lawrence Ricks, and Pfc. Joseph Sebock requested Carlson's permission to attempt a canoe escape to Australia. Carlson granted permission with the condition: "If you make it and we don't, tell them what happened." The three later reconsidered and stayed for the rest of the night.[27]

After determining the Raider force could not make it to the subs, Carlson posted a security detail. The men spotted a small party of Japanese and fired, killing three of them. The skirmish further strengthened Lieutenant Colonel Carlson's miscalculation of an enemy that by now barely existed. To make matters worse, Carlson had not seen Major Roosevelt in some time. He asked his officers what his next move should be.

Although it is not clear who suggested surrender, it is clear that Carlson endorsed an attempt to surrender to the Japanese forces on Makin.[28] Carlson sent out Capt. Ralph H. Coyte and his runner, Pvt. William McCall, to make contact with the enemy forces and deliver a surrender note written by Captain Coyte.[29] This task proved to be difficult because only a dozen of the island's defenders were still alive.

Surprisingly Captain Coyte and his runner McCall were able to find a living Japanese soldier and pass along the message without getting killed. The Japanese soldier they passed the message to, however, was shot soon afterward. The message was most likely recovered by a Japanese force several days later.[30] Purportedly the note was used in a Tokyo Rose–type propaganda broadcast.[31] After the war, a copy of what is believed to be the note emerged in a Japanese monograph. The note read,

> Dear Sir,
>
> I am a member of the American forces now on Makin. We have suffered severe casualties and wish to make an end of the bloodshed and bombings. We wish to surrender according to the rules of military law and be treated as prisoners of war. We would also like to bury our dead and care for our wounded. There are approximately 60 of us left. We have all voted to surrender. I would like to see you personally as soon as possible to prevent future bloodshed and bombing.[32]

The surrender was not an order but rather an option. According to Sgt. Frank Joe Lawson, Carlson decided to stay with the wounded but told his men that those who wanted to could attempt to return to the submarines. With commander-endorsed permission, Sergeant Lawson and a Raider-filled a raft headed toward the surf.[33]

News of the surrender spread down through the Raider ranks. Pvt. Ben Carson, a member of the covering force that Lieutenant Colonel Carlson suggested left with him at 1930 hours, was still on the beach when he heard the news. He was told that it was "every man for himself."[34] Private Carson was amazed and disheartened at this news, and he immediately sent fellow guard Pvt. Sylvester Kuzniewski to ask Lieutenant Colonel Carlson if they could have a go at beating the waves.

Believing he had taken the covering force with him in his attempt to leave Makin, Lieutenant Colonel Carlson was shocked to see a Raider in dry clothes and gave his approval.[35] With the added motivation of surrender at hand, Ben Carson and his fellow boat mates made it through to the submarines.

Although Carson had come in on the *Argonaut*, he left on the *Nautilus*. For many returning Raiders, given the prospects of surrender, either submarine would do. Not long after going aboard the *Nautilus*, Carson says, he was given a drink by the doctor, and then he went straight to sleep.

Back on the island, Major Roosevelt rejoined Lieutenant Colonel Carlson, relieving the colonel of his second reason for surrender.[36] At this time, 2nd Lt. Charles Lamb first heard of the surrender attempt:

> The first time that I heard the word "surrender" was when I was informed by Carlson in the presence of Roosevelt, that a surrender note had been written. I had left the area which normally would be called the Command Post to go on a brief foraging and reconnaissance trip. I encountered no enemy on this trip and acquired and brought back some Japanese beer. Evidently the details of the surrend[er]ing and the writing of the note had taken place while I was away.[37]

On the *Nautilus*, Commander Haines and Lieutenant Peatross heard about the ordeal on the beach from the few Raiders who arrived onboard after Peatross and his men. Peatross discussed the situation with the new arrivals and learned of their struggle to make it through the waves.[38] As he listened to stories of the desperation on the beach, Peatross couldn't help but become frustrated and feel helpless. He wondered why he and Carlson's force hadn't linked up given the fact that Peatross and his men had sometimes been "as close as 200 yards or less" from the main Raider body.[39]

Around 0700 the next morning the *Nautilus* moved closer to the beach in an attempt to lessen the Raiders' load. At 0719 the submarine picked up Sergeant Lawson's boat. From Lawson

Peatross heard the story of the "surrender." Peatross, still concerned about the situation on shore, had asked Commander Haines several times to allow him to take a rescue party back to the island. With Lawson's news of an attempted surrender, Commander Haines finally relented and allowed Lieutenant Peatross to send five of the best swimmers back in a raft.

The volunteer rescue party consisted of Sgts. Robert V. Allard and Dallas H. Cook, Pfc. Richard N. Olbert, and Pvts. Donald R. Roberton and John I. Kerns. Their mission was to help the Raiders with extra motors and fuel and give Lieutenant Colonel Carlson the following message from Commander Haines: "We are going to stay here until we get every living Raider off that island, and if we have to, we'll send every able-bodied man ashore, sailors included."[40] Although these men had just survived the battle on the island and then the ordeal of making it to the submarines, they readily volunteered to return.[41]

Shortly after the rescue boat shoved off from the *Nautilus*, the *Argonaut* dove. The *Nautilus* followed the *Argonaut* and stayed under for a half hour. At 0900 the *Nautilus* resurfaced but had to dive again upon spotting Japanese aircraft on the radar. According to Lieutenant Peatross, the duty officer on the periscope had seen a rubber boat being bombed and strafed. The men aboard the *Nautilus* assumed the five-man rescue party had been killed.[42]

According to Lieutenant Colonel Carlson's report, the boat arrived at the reef and from there shot a line to the shore. Carlson also mentions a man swimming to shore and relaying Commander Haines's message that the subs would remain off the island until the Raiders were evacuated. Whether this man was part of the rescue party or not is unclear.[43] If he was a member of the rescue crew, it can be assumed that he swam back to the boat because, according to Carlson, the boat was strafed and "nothing more was seen of it or its crew."[44]

While Lieutenant Colonel Carlson had desperately wanted to leave the island with the Raiders on the seventeenth, contrary to the belief of the men on the *Nautilus*, Carlson was not in a hurry to leave on the eighteenth. Although Carlson later stated, in his report, that on the eighteenth it was his duty to "remain until the last man was evacuated,"[45] salvaging the mission rather than regrouping seems to have been the first order of the day.

The morning of the eighteenth brought Lieutenant Colonel Carlson the realization, through the natives, that only a handful of Japanese remained scattered on the island. This bit of intelligence heartened Carlson to attempt to accomplish the mission's original goals, and Carlson sent men across the island to burn and destroy the Japanese defenses and supplies. The Raiders found weapons and clothes along the beach and set out to "mop up Makin."[46]

Japanese aircraft bombed the island throughout the day, but only Japanese defenses were harmed. Carlson set up a headquarters at the Government House and stockpiled some food. He also swept across the island to account for the dead and gather intelligence.[47] Carlson found fourteen Raiders and eighty-three Japanese dead.[48] The remains of eleven of the fourteen Raiders were found on the northern end of the island and the other three Raider dead were Peatross's men. Carlson and his party also managed to set fire to nearly one thousand barrels of aviation fuel.[49]

Communication with the submarines had been almost non-existent since the raid had begun. Like the raft motors, the radios were woefully inadequate. Pvt. Kenneth McCullough was the only radioman still on the island, and Carlson soon made good use of him.[50] While the radios did not work, McCullough could still signal by blinker. He arranged for the subs to pick up the Raiders at the calm lagoon at Flink Point at 2130.

Short on boats, the Raiders borrowed native outrigger canoes and loaded the wounded on boats that had been lashed together. When the boats were ready to shove off, Carlson was found asleep near a flagpole and was awakened by Second Lieutenant Lamb.[51] At this point Carlson began insisting that he stay and organize the natives in resistance against the Japanese; he was taken to the boat by Lamb.[52] Carlson and his weary armada set off for the submarines, a full twenty-four hours after their first attempt to reach the submarines.

Although the pickup time was arranged for 2130, the Raider procession did not make it through the lagoon to the *Nautilus* for another two hours. Peatross later noted that he had never seen such "a motley looking group of humans" as the men who finally arrived from the beach. He also noticed that although it had been only forty-three hours since Peatross had dropped off Lieutenant Colonel Carlson with A Company, Carlson looked as though he'd aged ten years.[53] The *Nautilus* commander, Haines, reported the last Raiders' arrival in his after-action report as well as Lieutenant Colonel Carlson's assurances that all Raiders had been evacuated:

> Proceeded as requested and received the remainder of the Raider unit on board at 2330. The commanding officer of the Raider unit reported to the group commander that he was satisfied that all surviving personnel of his command had been evacuated from the island.[54]

With Lieutenant Colonel Carlson's assurances that all men were aboard, the *Argonaut* and *Nautilus* set off for Pearl Harbor, leaving Makin Island in their wakes. As the Raider-filled submarines slipped beneath the sea and sped back to the safer waters of Hawaii, Makin Island still showed signs that the Raiders had been there. Many of the island's coconut trees were split in half by the bombs and bullets of the battle. What had been the island's major buildings were now destroyed. Japanese ships and planes lay dead in the water, and aviation fuel was burning on the island. The Raiders had left their mark on the Japanese outpost.

The natives did not forget the perhaps most memorable two days of their lives and recalled for years to come the day the "submarines" (Raiders) had fought the Japanese on their island. But aside from the destruction of battle, the Raiders had left behind something else that the natives discovered shortly after the Americans' departure. Not the results of U.S. might, or uniforms or rubber boats. Not anything that Lieutenant Colonel Carlson knew he had left behind. If Carlson had realized his mistake, he certainly would have turned the subs around.[56] In the midst of the confusion of what was later referred to as "the most spectacular commando operation of the Pacific War," nine Americans had been left on Makin alive.[57]

Chapter Three

CONFLICTING REPORTS

The full story of the Makin raid probably will never be recorded in its entirety except in the Book of Time for the archives of the Great Historian. Undoubtedly, most of the various reports on this action were colored to some extent by individuals due to personalities involved, influence of newspaper and magazine articles, books, and last but by no means least, loyalty to the Marine Corps.

LT. COL. CHARLES T. LAMB, USMC (RET.),
FORMER SECOND MARINE RAIDER BATTALION OFFICER[1]

U pon their return from Makin, the Raiders were immediately greeted with the Navy's approval through awards and promotions. In fact, several Raiders were promoted before the submarines returned to Hawaii.[2] The Navy's report of a stealthy attack on the unsuspecting Japanese had given the press and the American people the good news they had been waiting for.

With Makin, the Navy now had its own version of the Doolittle raid.

Newspapers, naval monographs, and later historians reported that the raid went exactly as planned.[3] Soon the words *gung ho* and *Carlson's Raiders* entered the American vocabulary and the Makin raid became a morale boost for a nation hungry for retribution. The enemy had been wiped out, installations were destroyed, enemy reinforcements were annihilated, and the Raiders had returned victorious.

On paper, the accounts of the raid's successful results, coupled with Japanese flags and battle souvenirs, gave those at home tangible evidence of what happened on the raid. Also on paper, however, the Navy alluded to the true story of the raid and its mishaps. Although the Navy had no knowledge of Marine Raiders being left behind at the time, the comments of Navy leadership left no doubt that such a tragedy could have occurred. In fact, these comments are prophetic and incriminating historical records of the realities of the raid. Histories have left the impression that the raid's mishaps and Carlson's ill-fated decisions were revealed after initial reports had been written. The after-action reports make it clear, however, that privately the Navy quickly realized that some of the bravest men in Marine Corps history had been let down and that the Navy had narrowly avoided a complete disaster.

The reports of task unit and Raider commander Lieutenant Colonel Carlson and task group commander Haines were submitted shortly after the raid. After reviewing these reports, the commander of the Pacific Fleet Submarines, Rear Adm. R. H. English, submitted a report to commander in chief of the Pacific Fleet Admiral Nimitz. The final report was submitted by Admiral Nimitz to the commander in chief of the U.S. Fleet, Adm. Ernest J. King.

Under the heading "Operations on Makin, August 17–18,

1942," Lieutenant Colonel Carlson provided his account of the events on Makin Island. Unfortunately, in this report he did not address those events that most likely led to the confusion of the night of the seventeenth. Lieutenant Colonel Carlson's description of the night as "the spiritual low point of the expedition" was the closest he came to addressing the nocturnal command breakdown.[4] He made no attempt to explain either his poor leadership on that night or the results of his command decisions. Rather, Carlson described the unattractive aspects of the mission with euphemisms:

> Finally, I would invite the attention of all military leaders to the illustration provided by our situation at Makin on the night of August 17th which emphasizes truth that is as old as the military profession: no matter how bad your own situation may appear to be, there is always the possibility that the situation of the enemy is much worse.[5]

The situation that Carlson faced on Makin was by no means ideal or desirable. Shore-to-boat communication was unreliable at best. The surf was insurmountable and the ordeal was exacerbated by faulty equipment. Many of the actions Carlson took to meet these challenges, however, compounded the desperation of the Raiders' predicament. Lieutenant Colonel Carlson's miscalculation of the number of remaining enemy was his basis for an early withdrawal, an attempted surrender to a barely existent enemy, and the "every man for himself" fever that spread throughout the battalion. Carlson's overestimation was also the source of the raid's disorganization and quite possibly the reason nine men were abandoned.

Carlson chose not to mention the surrender note in his report or the desperation that followed his decision to surrender. No matter how vague his references to the events, his report made clear that something happened on the seventeenth that he did not want to relive on paper. Instead of coming to terms with his inaccurate assessment of the situation on Makin and the events that resulted from that assessment, Carlson placed the blame on, or rather gave credit to, the boldness of the few enemy soldiers who were left:

> Although the mission of destruction of enemy forces and installations had not been completed, after the last bombing the Raider commander decided to withdraw according to plan. The appointed time of departure was approaching and he considered that it was necessary to fall back slowly so as to permit an orderly embarkation into the boats. It appears that there were only a few Japanese soldiers left alive, yet such is the effect of boldness in a few resolute men that it seemed to the Raider commander at this time that he was still opposed by a large force.[6]

An encounter that Pvt. Ben Carson had with Lieutenant Colonel Carlson on the *Nautilus* after the raid gives some explanation to this omission. When Private Carson's boat returned to the sub, he took the "medicine" (alcohol) the doctor gave him and then went straight to sleep. Unbeknownst to Private Carson, he had fallen asleep in the officers' section of the *Nautilus*. He was awakened by the voices of Lieutenant Colonel Carlson and Captain Coyte, his company commander. Carson still remembers seeing the two men in the blue light of the submarine discussing what was at that point the most embarrassing aspect of the mission. According to Carson, the two men were talking about what they were going to do about the surrender note. At about this time they saw Private Carson lying in the bunk and ordered him to leave the room. It was apparent to Ben Carson that the surrender incident would be covered up.[7]

The attempted surrender soon became unmentionable among the Raiders. Lieutenant Peatross, who had received word of the surrender from Raiders arriving on the *Nautilus*, was curious about the episode and talked with several witnesses who verified the attempt. To his surprise, however, Lieutenant Colonel Carlson did not mention the surrender in his briefing after the raid. Given the nature of the gung-ho meetings and the Raiders' belief that anything could be questioned, Peatross was surprised that Carlson never mentioned the surrender note.[8]

Private McCall, who delivered the surrender note, has since stated that Lieutenant Colonel Carlson ordered him not to discuss the surrender.[9] Captain Coyte confirmed McCall's story, saying that Lieutenant Colonel Carlson had returned the captain's after-action report and said that the report should be rewritten based on Admiral Nimitz's request that any reference to the surrender be deleted.[10]

Blankfort's autobiography of Carlson, *The Big Yankee*, mentions a "suggested" surrender. According to the book, on the night of the seventeenth a young private, who was exasperated, asked an officer, "Why don't we surrender?" One of Lieutenant Colonel Carlson's NCOs slapped the Raider for making the suggestion, and Carlson walked away, deducing that surrender was not necessary.[11] Like Carlson's report, his biography omits the actual stories of both the attempted surrender and the command breakdown that followed.

Although Lieutenant Colonel Carlson's report did not mention the surrender note, it was clear on the number of Raiders he believed were killed during the raid. Lieutenant Colonel Carlson wrote that the number of Raider dead on Makin was fourteen. Carlson also assumed in his report that the five-man rescue party was killed in the water, bringing his number of dead to nineteen:

The boat was strafed and nothing more was seen of it or of the crew. . . . Our own dead on this northern front numbered eleven, including my intelligence officer, Lieutenant Holtom, who had been up on the right flank looking for me. Our other three men killed in action were members of Lieutenant Peatross' boat crew, which landed behind the enemy lines to the south.[12]

In truth, eighteen Raiders were later confirmed dead and twelve were confirmed missing. How Lieutenant Colonel Carlson calculated that all living Raiders were off the island is not known. How and when Carlson established a definitive figure on Raider dead and missing are not exactly clear either. The counting was most likely done in Hawaii and not on Makin. When Lieutenant Colonel Carlson arrived on the *Nautilus*, he gave Commander Haines the assurance that all Raiders had left the island.[13] None of the after-action reports indicated that anyone doubted Carlson. There is also no record of a muster report being conducted between the subs from the time they left Makin until they reached Hawaii.

After the raid, Lieutenant Peatross, with the other men on the *Nautilus*, tried to tally the dead and missing, but according to Peatross, the actual numbers were not sorted out until the Raiders were back at Camp Catlin.[14] Eventually it was decided that eighteen men could be confirmed dead; fifteen were confirmed dead in the northern area of the island alone. At least two Raider eyewitnesses were needed to confirm that a Raider was in fact dead. This still left twelve Raiders missing in action (MIA). It was assumed that five of the twelve missing were the rescue party that was last seen on the morning of the eighteenth. The other seven men were believed to have died in the surf while attempting to return to the subs.[15]

Despite Carlson's claim that the Raiders controlled the

island on the eighteenth and his comment that it was his duty to "remain until the last man was evacuated," Carlson had counted the number of dead on the island incorrectly.[16] Although Carlson counted fourteen dead Raiders on the island, the Raiders confirmed that fifteen were killed in the northern area of the island alone.[17]

When Lieutenant Colonel Carlson first responded to reports that nine Raiders had been left behind, he stated that he had personally checked the bodies of eighteen Raiders before he left Makin: "There can be no question about the eighteen that were killed in action, for I checked their bodies. The twelve 'missing' were presumed to have been lost in the surf during the first night attempt at evacuation and during the strafing of the boat the following morning."[18] Lieutenant Colonel Carlson's later statements are in conflict with his after-action report and point directly to the obvious; that is, when Carlson left Makin Island, he did not have a correct count of his dead or missing and would not have the correct count of missing until he returned to Hawaii.

It is clear that Lieutenant Colonel Carlson was unwilling to come to terms with the effects that his overestimation of the enemy had on the decisions he made. He was also unwilling to acknowledge the lack of command and control that existed during the raid once the Raiders learned of his attempt to surrender.

Like Carlson, Commander Haines, in his own report, did not detail the ugly side of the raid. Although Haines did not leave the *Nautilus* during the mission, as commander of the task group, he heard accounts of the events on Makin shortly after they occurred.[19] In his after-action report, Haines did not delve into these accounts, but unlike Carlson, he did report what he witnessed to be the raid's faults. He presented a mission that was flawed as a direct result of the commander's actions. In fact, although his report was a preface to his recommendations for awards, it reads like a recommendation for demotion. Unlike Lieutenant Colonel Carlson, Rear Admiral English, and Admiral Nimitz, Haines felt that the mission was not the success that had been hoped for and that the losses were greater than had been anticipated.[20]

Commander Haines's report drew attention to several aspects of the mission that in hindsight provide some explanation for the difficulties that led to the nine Raiders' ordeal. Perhaps one of the most interesting details his report offers was his own discomfort with the decisions his superiors made concerning the group's organization. Haines claims that planning and training suffered as a result of the organizational setup of the mission. Calling the setup "bad practice," the task group commander came out strongly against the lack of coordinated planning and the undistributed load placed on the senior officers of each section.[21] Further, according to Commander Haines, he was designated as commander of the expedition only five days before the Raiders set sail.

Commander Haines's report further made it evident that he believed that the expedition suffered because it lacked the proper staff to plan and work through the mission's complexities. The commander brings Lieutenant Colonel Carlson to bear on the mistake of miscalculating the enemy force. Haines seemed to blame Lieutenant Colonel Carlson's poor assessment of the situation at Makin on the lieutenant colonel's background in guerrilla warfare.[22] In Haines's eyes, while Carlson viewed the raid as guerrilla warfare, he did not plan or execute it as such. The task group commander admonished Carlson for planning the impossible task of rendezvousing in the water. The commander describes Carlson's planning as "too detailed and too inflexible." The plan's inflexibility was, according to Haines, "an invitation to catastrophe."[23] Similar veiled references to what could easily have gone wrong are peppered throughout Haines's report and the final report of Admiral Nimitz. These glimpses into the failures of the mission's training and leadership represent a shadow of the catastrophe that the Navy brass thought they had averted.

The mission was not only lacking in adequate planning, according to Commander Haines. The Raiders' training prior to the mission was inadequate as well. Lieutenant Colonel Carlson took pride in his "well-trained" Raiders, and he believed training was the key to a successful raid. The disembarkation problems that were encountered from the beginning, though, raised questions as to whether or not the Raiders had been adequately prepared for the mission. Although the mission was under the Navy's command, the Navy was quick to point the finger at Carlson.

Carlson's biography states that "countless practice landings were made from the subs" a month before the raid on Makin.[24] This account is partially backed up by Admiral Nimitz's report, which references the "several night landings on Oahu from submarines."[25] This is contrary however, to Peatross's account of the training. Peatross cites the dress rehearsal as the only time the unit as a whole trained with the submarines.[26] Raider Ben Carson agrees that the Raiders were exposed to subs only once before the mission. Carson asserts that the rehearsal was a quick dive on the *Argonaut* on the night of August 6 to see if anyone was claustrophobic and how hot the sub would get when packed with Raiders.[27]

Whether there was one rehearsal or many, task group commander Haines stresses that there had not been enough. Even in the words preceding his praise of the raid and recommendations for awards, Commander Haines stated that there was a "lack of opportunity for adequate preparation and training" for the mission.[28] Haines felt that "more day and night rehearsal of approach, launching of boats, landing and recovery, are very much in order." Commander Haines further addressed the raft fiasco, which, he wrote, "almost resulted in disaster." Haines pointed out the lack of proper training with rafts: "Another suggestion is that the Marines, who were largely self-taught in the handling of their rubber boats in the surf, be furnished the most experienced instructors available from such sources as the Navy, Coast Guard, and Hawaiian surf-men."[29]

Haines's frustrations with the faults of the mission, his superiors, and Lieutenant Colonel Carlson are betrayed in his report. Because he was charged as commander of the task group but was not charged with the training of the men, he felt responsible for the mission's failings in an area that Carlson had sole control over. The raft ordeal had not left his, or any other Raider's, mind. Neither had he forgotten the mission's teetering on the brink of disaster. Thus, he repeatedly stressed that he was not to blame for the Raider's insufficient training and blamed his higher command for the flawed organizational setup.

In the brief report of the commander of the Pacific Fleet Submarines, Admiral English took issue with Commander Haines's report. English disagreed with Haines's assessment of the mission's organizational structure.[30] He wrote that he could not concur with Commander Haines that it was bad practice to charge the senior officers with the planning, organization, and training of their respective units. Admiral English did concede, however, that as much night rehearsal and training as time permitted should have been conducted.

Admiral Nimitz's report began with comments directly criticizing the raid's disorganized start. The admiral stated that the enemy could have stopped the whole mission by attacking the Raiders before they hit the beach: "Raiders landing without organization on the beach might have been stopped by a single machine gun."[31]

Admiral Nimitz glossed over the situation Carlson was dropped into as well as the poor equipment the Navy provided for the mission. He also minimized Haines's comments on the Raiders' training by citing the Raider battalion's "extensive training" before the mission.[32] Additionally Admiral Nimitz criticized Carlson's use of caution in the offensive operation. Nimitz accused Carlson, a guerrilla warfare expert and commander of a highly trained commando unit, of not attacking aggressively enough. According to Nimitz, the Raider commander's reluctance to push forward debilitated the mission.

> The raiding force cannot let itself be tied down by position fighting. It must maintain mobility, striking rapidly, seeking to surprise and rout the enemy before they can recover and organize defenses. Should the force be pinned down by a "fire fight", it must continue offensive reconnaissance instead of retreating or remaining static. After the first part of the engagement, the Raider force did not strike aggressively; for example, the platoon on the left flank suffered no casualties and made slow progress.[33]

Admiral Nimitz's words on aggressiveness were mild in relation to his comments on how things should have gone. He literally underlined Lieutenant Colonel Carlson's failure to take the offensive. The admiral then proceeded to provide a litany of ways the mission would have been different if Carlson had been aggressive, to include fewer Raider casualties:

> The old story in war of the *importance of the offensive* was again demonstrated. On the afternoon of August 17, had the raiding force sent out reconnaissance patrols and pushed forward instead of withdrawing, they would have discovered that the apparent heavy resistance was the fire

of only a handful of men fighting to the death. They could have destroyed installations on the island and reembarked at their leisure, probably saving most of the loss of life from drowning and from strafing by planes on 18 August.[34]

With these comments on what could have been, Nimitz implied that Carlson was responsible for the Raiders that did not return. The admiral speculated that had Carlson pushed forward on the seventeenth, he would have realized the enemy forces had been destroyed and the fear of a counterattack, which drove the Raiders' desperation to get off the island, would not have existed.

While the tone and substance of each of the reports revealed the actual failures of the raid, each writer's final assessment suggested that the Makin raid could not have gone better. Despite Admiral Nimitz's biting comments and the clear faults laid out by Commander Haines, the Navy made the best of the mission's results when it had to, in the desperate times of war.

In fact, several lines of the reports read like descriptions of a bungled mission, but all ended in recommendations for awards and with lines of praise. In his report to Admiral King, Admiral Nimitz wrote that the raid "succeeded in all its purposes." Rear Admiral English wrote that the raid was remarkable and that "the results obtained were so nearly those that were planned." English also felt the expedition reached "a successful conclusion."[35]

The Navy's attempts to whitewash the facts are further revealed in World War II Marine combat correspondent Samuel E. Stavisky's account of the raid. In the summer of 1942 *Washington Post* reporter turned war correspondent Stavisky was anxiously waiting in San Francisco to be deployed to the action in the Pacific. Eager to report, he set about interviewing U.S. casualties recovering in a naval hospital.

Stavisky had read accounts of the Makin raid's success in the papers, so when he learned that some of the Raiders were in the hospital he was determined to interview them. His interest in the story grew when he was told that the Makin Raiders were off-limits for interviews. After convincing high-ranking Marine public relations officers and the base commander, Stavisky was granted permission to conduct interviews with half a dozen wounded Second Marine Raiders.[36] According to Stavisky, the men were just glad to have made it off Makin alive.[37]

Stavisky was shocked by the Raiders' version of the events, especially the attempted surrender:

> I had seen the headlines in San Francisco and had read the stirring story of the commando raid by the Second. I was dumbfounded, then, by the startling, differing version told by the men I interviewed. I talked to six, and each individually swore he was there in the council of war that decided on surrender. The Raiders, elite of the Corps, willing to surrender rather than fight to the death! Unbelievable! Nonetheless, I had to accept the unpleasant truth, confirmed by the half dozen participants.[38]

Aware of the stark contradiction between the Navy's account and that of the men who participated in the raid, Stavisky knew his interview would never be printed: "I also, thinking it over, had to accept the unpleasant fact that none of the armed services' censors would, or could, let this disturbing account leak out into public knowledge. I didn't give the censors a chance to kill this incredible story. I killed the story myself. Why get another reprimand?"[39]

The Navy, even while praising the raid in public and in its reports, knew that more Marines were not killed on the raid because of the courage of the men themselves. Accounts and reports of the raid make clear that the disorganized situation directly led to dangerous self-initiated acts of bravery that would have otherwise been unnecessary.

Chapter Four

THE LEFT BEHIND

*Ashore the only indication of life came from the billow-
ing flames of the gasoline fire.*

LIEUTENANT COLONEL CARLSON ON LEAVING MAKIN[1]

A few days after returning to Hawaii, Lieutenant Colonel
Carlson called the Raiders together for a memorial service
for the men who had died on Makin. Carlson spoke of the burial
arrangements he had made before he left Makin, and he also
spoke fondly of the men who had died on Makin:

> Moreover, they are still with us in spirit—will always be
> with us. Allard, with his boyish smile, Johnson, with his
> strange scowl. . . . It is not possible to render honor to
> these fallen comrades on the field of battle. I did what I
> could. I went to each as he lay with his face towards the
> enemy. I placed each on his back that he might rest more

easily, and I said a silent prayer over each. With the native Gilbertese I arranged for each to be given a Christian burial. And so, they lie there today, in that soil of that delightful South Pacific isle, beneath the palms under which they won their victory.[2]

What the Raider commander did not know was that, as he was paying homage to Sergeant Allard and his boyish smile, Allard was trying to stay alive. It is doubtful that "delightful" is the word Allard would have used to describe the island he and the eight other Raiders had been left on. The "victory" Lieutenant Colonel Carlson spoke of was not felt by the nine prisoners of the Japanese in the Central Pacific. Sergeant Allard and the eight other Raider prisoners were on their way to the Imperial Japanese Navy's Sixth Base Headquarters on Kwajalein Island. They would soon be in the custody of the man who had sent the reinforcements to Makin to combat the raid, Vice Adm. Koso Abe.

The Japanese reinforcements had not discovered the nine abandoned Raiders immediately. In fact, according to Japanese records, they did not capture the Raiders until August 24, 1942, five days after the Raider battalion's departure and four days after the arrival of Abe's troops. The nine men left behind evaded capture until they had nowhere else to go. With submarines miles from Makin and nothing left but the remnants of battle, the island must have been a lonely place for the nine Marine Raiders on August 18, 1942.

The thoughts and fears that ran through the minds of these nine men upon realizing that they had been abandoned are too tragic to suppose. With nowhere to go and few options, that third night on Makin must have been ten times worse than the previous night's fiasco. In an unfortunate twist of fate, it is likely that five of the nine had left the safety of the *Nautilus* earlier that morning as the rescue party that had returned to Makin to tell Lieutenant Colonel Carlson that the submarines would not leave until every Raider was off the island.

The journal of a Makin islander, George Noran, gives perhaps the only known insight into what happened on the island after the raid and the condition of these abandoned Raiders. The Raiders' arrival on Makin greatly affected the lives of the islanders. According to Noran, several islanders were killed in the Japanese bombing raids. Each time Noran described the noise of the American submarines' firing and the Japanese bombs hitting the island he wrote, "I thought it was my last day to live." The islanders seem to have welcomed the Marines' arrival, however, and their brief liberation from Japanese rule. The Butaritarians helped themselves to the dead Japanese soldiers' bicycles and saki.[3]

Noran made it clear that he knew the Americans were not there to hurt the islanders. He assured one fellow islander that the Marines wouldn't "shoot them." According to Noran, after the Raider force left Makin, the Japanese bombed the island for a third day in a row. Some time after the bombing, "one big aeroplane," as Noran recalls, came and brought more Japanese soldiers.[4] The plane was most likely a Kawanishi flying boat.

The Japanese reinforcements told an elder of the island tribe to bring all the bicycles back to the Japanese. Noran grabbed a bicycle he had confiscated from a dead Japanese soldier and began to take it back when he saw another Japanese plane arriving. He wrote that he did not pay attention to the plane because he knew the Japanese had already landed.[5] However, he was caught off guard by what he saw next:

> But we were surprised when we saw four men in one of the native hut, and when looked at them they pointed at the plane and make signs with their hands to tell us to

come to them. And when we came near to them we saw that they were American soldiers. I wondered how didn't the Japanese see them; and the Japanese soldiers passed them, about half an hour before us. Then we went to them and asked them where they will go. They said that they will broom all the Japanese away from Butaritari and beside that they told us that they were very hungry. They told us to get them some coco-nuts. Then I told one native boy that was with me to get some coco-nuts for them. But before that native boy climbed a tree I told that the Japanese has already gone to Butaritari village. When they heard this, they stopped and told the native boy not to get coco-nuts. Then they asked me which way did the Japanese went. I told them that they went to Butaritari Village to search the American soldiers. When these Americans heard this they told us to go back to Hen Village and they went after the Japs.[6]

This description of the hungry Raiders evading capture on small, triangular Makin Island is disheartening. Unfortunately, the Raiders' situation only worsened. Noran's journal seems to indicate that the men might have been split up for some time; it is unclear when they reunited.

According to Noran, this was not the only encounter the islanders had with the left-behind Raiders. The Raiders seemed to cause quite a stir on the island; an argument between two natives over the abandoned Raiders even led to a murder. Noran recorded that the nine Americans told a native boy named Takanu that they wanted to see the Father, the Catholic priest on Makin. The islander relayed the message to the Father and also told another native named Na Buaka about the Americans. Na Buaka, fearing for the priest's safety, scolded Takanu for sending the man to the Americans. Takanu assured Na

Buaka that the Americans only wanted to ask the priest about the Japanese.[7]

Although Noran did not indicate whether or not the priest met with the Raiders, other raid histories claim that the Raiders met with the Makin priest and that he negotiated the nine Raiders' surrender to the Japanese.[8] This, however, was not the case. In fact, a May 13, 1946, letter from the commander of the Marianas to Headquarters U.S. Army Forces, Middle Pacific, states that the priest on Makin at the time, Father Guchard of the Mission of the Sacred Heart, the French Catholic Society, did not see any of the Marines. Father Guchard did say that the natives told him that nine Marines were left stranded on Makin.[9]

Unconvinced by Takanu's arguments that the Americans would not hurt the priest, Na Buaka accused Takanu of putting the Father to death. The two quarreled, and the priest came and broke up the fight. Later that evening, a drunken and insulted Takanu returned and stabbed Na Buaka to death. The Makin islanders tied up Takanu for his crime, and the Japanese took the murderer, kept him tied, and fed him his food on the ground like a dog.[10]

The island murder coincided with the Japanese cleanup of Makin. Noran wrote that two days after he saw the Raiders, a ship brought a thousand or more Japanese soldiers to the island. Upon arriving, the soldiers told the island tribe's elder, Mr. Kansaki, to order the natives "to dig one big grave for the American soldiers" killed during the raid. Japanese records report that the bodies of twenty-one Marine Raiders were found on Makin.[11] Noran wrote that some of the dead Marines were found drowned on the beach. The Japanese burned their own dead and sent the ashes back to Japan.[12]

After the islanders dug the communal grave and buried the Marines, the Japanese brought Takanu to the site and made him sit by the Marines' grave.[13] The Japanese put a handkerchief over the murderer's eyes, and an officer came and told him he would be killed for committing murder. The Japanese told all the natives in the area that they would also be killed if they committed murder. The officer then beheaded Takanu and placed his body with the Marines'.

Captured Japanese records validate Noran's story of the Japanese reinforcements arriving by plane. According to the documents thirty-three Japanese soldiers flew into the atoll on August 20, 1942.[14] Statements of former Japanese officers confirm Noran's mention of the arrival of a ship that carried Japanese soldiers to Makin: "The commander of the Sixth Base Force then made preparations to send vessels and land combat units as platoons, two machine gun platoons and two anti-tank guns, drawn from units stationed in the Marshall area. They were to land within Makin Atoll at 1300 hours on 20 August under cover of the 65th Subchaser Division but reached Makin at 100 hours on 21 August, one day later than scheduled, only to find the enemy had already withdrawn from the island."[15]

This was not the first time that American attacks had affected the Sixth Base Force commander, Vice Admiral Abe. Six months earlier, two-carrier task forces totaling two aircraft carriers, five cruisers, and ten destroyers had attacked Kwajalein and other Marshall islands. The attack succeeded in killing the Kwajalein commander, and Vice Admiral Abe arrived on Kwajalein on February 1, 1942, to replace him.[16]

On the day Abe became the Kwajalein commander, two Navy TBD-1 aircraft were shot down and crashed over Jaluit and six American airmen were taken prisoner. The POWs were sent to Kwajalein from Jaluit, and Admiral Abe forwarded them on to Japan.[17] This was the last time American prisoners left Kwajalein alive while Admiral Abe was commander.

Kwajalein Island had not been won during Japan's recent expansion. The Japanese had taken control of Kwajalein Atoll from the Germans in 1914, before World War I. Thus the installations and defenses were not makeshift. The Japanese had been steadily building up the two-mile island, which was located in the world's largest atoll, since it had become a part of the Japanese Empire. Kwajalein was the key to Japanese power in the Marshalls. The Japanese had placed more than one hundred Korean laborers on Kwajalein for manpower, and it was even home to several enslaved "comfort women."[18] The Marshall Islands were significant Japanese possessions and as such became strategic targets for the United States years before World War II.[19]

A Marine Corps monograph describes Kwajalein in the 1940s as a "green, palm covered island, composed of sand and coral, with the usual offshore reefs."[20] Although this description reads as if it comes from a travel brochure, Kwajalein was anything but a vacation spot. The island had been closed to foreigners for years before the war and was a now a vital communications and submarine base.[21] It was also the home of the Sixty-first Guard Unit, which in time became the captor of American MIAs in the Marshalls.

Because the Navy assumed the left-behind Raiders were dead, no Navy rescue planes searched for them as they were transported to Kwajalein. And plans for getting these condemned men back to the United States were not being made in Hawaii.

Who were the nine Raiders left behind? The exhumation of their graves fifty-seven years after their burial helped narrow down the possibilities. In November 1999 a U.S. Army Central Identification Laboratory, Hawaii (CILHI), team recovered the remains of nineteen Marine Raiders and one Pacific islander from Makin Island, and CILHI later identified the Marines' remains. The names of eighteen of the nineteen Marines identified were consistent with the eighteen confirmed dead by the Raiders upon their muster in Hawaii. The nineteenth identified Marine, Pvt. Carlyle O. Larson, was one on the Raiders' list of those missing and believed dead.[22]

Japanese records report that the bodies of twenty-one Marine Raiders were found on Makin and buried. The two additional Raiders were most likely buried in a different location on Makin. CILHI's 1999 recovery was not the Army's first attempt to recover the Raiders' remains. In 1948 an American Graves Registration team searched an area that had, according to Father Guchard, been the burial place of five Marines. Although the search yielded negative results, it is possible that the last two Marines were buried in this area.

Raider statements provide the most plausible identity of the two unrecovered Raiders. Raider Glenn Lincoln saw Texas native Pvt. Cletus Smith die as they proceeded up the island on the morning of August 17. Lincoln could not get to Smith's body because of the ensuing battle but tried to keep pigs that arrived on the scene from eating the Marine's remains. Japanese bullets hindered his attempts to preserve Smith, however.[23] Because two Raiders were necessary to confirm a Raider as killed in action, Smith was listed as MIA.

The second unrecovered Raider was most likely twenty-three-year old Cpl. James William Beecher from Appling County, Georgia. One Raider claims to have witnessed Beecher's body floating in the ocean, apparently mauled by sharks.[24]

The other remaining MIA Raiders—Pvt. Alden C. Mattison, Pfcs. Richard E. Davis and William E. Pallesen, and Cpl. James Gifford and the five men of the rescue party, Sgts. Robert V. Allard and Dallas H. Cook, Pfc. Richard N. Olbert, and Pvts. John I. Kerns and Donald R. Roberton—were mostly likely the nine men captured by the Japanese. The five-man rescue party was last seen just before its boat was strafed and overturned. It is highly possible that the current carried these men to another area of the island. Corporal Gifford and Private Mattison's last known whereabouts are uncertain. Private First Class Pallesen, however, was last seen battling the surf on the night of the seventeenth. Private First Class Davis was on the beach on the morning of the eighteenth but was not seen again. Raider Glenn Lincoln said he woke up near Davis on the beach: "On waking up in the morning I discovered that I was sharing a little dirt pocket with Private Dick Davis and Major Roosevelt. Dick was very upset and kept repeating, 'What's my aunt in Minneapolis going to say when she hears about this?' The major was upset, too, as he had lost his glasses in the surf and apparently couldn't see without them."[25]

Sadly, it seems that Corporal Gifford began and ended his life "left behind." Raider Kenneth Merrill recalled that after the Raiders returned from Makin Island, he took Gifford's billfold out of his seabag so that he could personally return it to his family. Like Gifford, Merrill was from Arizona. When he returned home on furlough, he traveled to Cornville, Arizona, where Corporal Gifford's mother ran the only general store in town. According to Merrill, after he returned the billfold and Gifford's mother shed some tears, she asked Merrill if he knew Joe's full story. The mother related to Merrill that she had found Gifford as a baby under a mesquite tree. Gifford was an Apache twin and had been left there by his mother. Mrs. Gifford took him and raised him. Kenneth Merrill was a good friend of Cpl. Joe Gifford's and has never forgotten him.

Sergeant Allard is also remembered fondly. The Raiders had nicknamed him "Mallard," and according to Ben Carson, Allard was always quacking to make his fellow Marines laugh.[26] The surviving Raiders' memories of the missing are very personal, and the revelations of how the nine were captured and killed has made these memories even more painful.

As mentioned earlier, the details of how and precisely when

the nine Raiders found each other is not certain. It is clear, however, that on the day they were captured they were together. After managing to stay concealed on Makin for a few days, the Raiders made it over to Little Makin Island.[27] On Little Makin they spoke with an elderly French priest, Father Clivaz, who had been in the Gilbert Islands for decades. Father Clivaz offered the Raiders his outrigger canoe for escape. According to Father Clivaz, fearing the men might not make it back to Hawaii, he gave supreme unction to the four Catholics of the nine-man group.[28] After receiving their last rites, the men shoved off in the canoe. Shortly after this, Father Clivaz witnessed a Japanese ship intercept the Raider canoe and capture the men a few miles offshore.[29]

According to translated Japanese documents, the Raiders were captured on August 24, 1942. The ship transferring the men to Kwajalein left on August 30 and arrived on September 2, 1942. A Japanese navy veteran who was on the ship that transported the Raiders to Kwajalein remembers the Raiders saying "Tokyo."[30] It can be assumed the men were anticipating their destination. But unlike many American POWs, they would never see mainland Japan. Instead they were taken to a piece of Japan that in time became an execution island for Americans.

Chapter Five

VICTORS' JUSTICE

All I remember is that they were Marines captured on Makin. There were nine (9) of them. I believe they were all Americans.

Sixty-first Guard Unit Commander, Capt.
Yoshio Obara, Imperial Japanese Navy[1]

Generally speaking, unlike their German counterparts, the Japanese chose not to abide by the Geneva Convention's rules for dealing with prisoners of war. The Japanese felt that in previous wars they had been "generous" to their prisoners. Colonel Odashima, chief of the Japanese Prisoner of War Office during World War II, made Japan's intentions toward prisoners clear in a speech to Japanese citizenry titled "Concerning the Treatment of Prisoners of War": "The slate is wiped clean regarding the regulations concerning prisoners of war"[2]— that is, the Japanese would no longer follow the guidelines for

POW treatment laid out by the Geneva Convention. As a result, the United States was not notified when its men, including the nine Marine Raiders, were taken prisoner.

It has been suggested that the executive officer of the Second Marine Raider Battalion, Maj. James Roosevelt, was the first to learn what happened to the nine Raiders who were left behind after the Makin raid. He supposedly learned this when he landed again on Makin in 1943 with the Makin invasion force. Roosevelt is said to have talked with the islanders about the Raider burial site. The natives told him about the nine Raiders he and his battalion had left behind, and Roosevelt concluded that the nine had been eventually taken to Japan.[3]

Former Raider 2nd Lt. Charles Lamb claimed that Japanese propaganda caused him to suspect Raiders had been left behind: "It was not until the Bouganville operation and as a result of propaganda from Japan that the horrible suspicion entered my mind that we had left living Marines on the island."[4] When the Navy first realized that nine Marines might have been left behind is not known. Records from the U.S. Navy war crimes investigation conducted in the Pacific shortly after Japan's surrender suggest that no official mention had been made of the missing Marines.

After the Japanese surrender, the task of investigating and prosecuting Japanese war criminals in the Pacific theater fell to the U.S. Pacific Fleet commander of the Marianas, Adm. George D. Murray. Admiral Murray issued a directive for war crimes to the director of the war crimes trials, Capt. John D. Murphy. After preliminary investigations, three trials for eighteen accused began in Quonset huts on Kwajalein Island on November 21, 1945.[5] Japanese naval officers were tried for the atrocities on Wake and other islands, but because few Japanese combatants survived on Kwajalein, conducting trials for atrocities on Kwajalein was a difficult matter.

Navy war crimes investigator Lt. Cdr. Nathan Finkelstein led the investigation of war crimes in the Marshall Islands. Because he did not know that Raiders had been left behind alive on Makin, the nine Marine Raiders were not a concern for Lieutenant Commander Finkelstein. The main focus of his Marshall Islands investigation was, in fact, the disappearance of three American bomber crews who were shot down over the Marshalls in late 1943 and early 1944.[6] Finkelstein and his staff had questioned everyone who could talk in the Marshalls, including Japanese officers, soldiers, and sailors. The only primary evidence available to the investigators were photos taken of two of the missing B-24 crews while they were in captivity. Japanese admiral Kamada had turned the photos over to the investigators upon his surrender. The photograph for the third missing B-24 crew was not found. Kamada insisted that he sent the third group to Kwajalein. The men under Kamada claimed that the crews were killed when U.S. forces bombed the ships transporting the POWs.

The investigators concluded that they did not have enough evidence to hold Kamada for the fliers' death; however, they also believed that the Japanese were withholding part of the story and that the men could have been killed rather than shipped to Kwajalein.[7] Marshallese witnesses, however, testified that crews meeting the descriptions of at least two of the missing crews made it to Kwajalein and were executed shortly after they arrived there.[8] Uncooperative Japanese officers, concocted stories, and nonspecific statements of well-meaning natives complicated the investigation, as did the similarity of the circumstances surrounding the three incidents, including the similar number of men missing in each case. All of this confusion was in fact a sign of how common an occurrence the shipment of American POWs to Kwajalein for execution was.

Unlike other Japanese-held islands, Kwajalein had fallen early in 1944. The few Japanese who were not killed in the American invasion were sent to Pearl Harbor for imprisonment.[9] The admiral in charge of the island at the time of the invasion, Rear Adm. Monzo Akiyama, was killed in the battle.[10]

With the American prisoners located miles from the area of investigation and the top-ranking officers from the island's garrison dead, finding someone responsible for executions in time for the Kwajalein trials was nearly impossible. Despite the evidence pointing to executions on Kwajalein, without immediate suspects to question, the United States couldn't convict the accused Japanese executioners at the trials.

Although the trials on Kwajalein did not find any of the Japanese officers and men guilty of the executions on Kwajalein, they inadvertently led to the discovery of the missing Raiders' fate. During a recess in one of the Kwajalein trials, Marshall islanders approached Navy prosecutor Lt. William P. Mahoney and told him that they had seen nine American soldiers beheaded on Kwajalein in the fall of 1942.[11] Lieutenant Mahoney was dumbfounded by the date the natives had given him. He could not imagine who would have been on Kwajalein in 1942 because Kwajalein was not bombed on a regular basis until almost a year later. Despite his doubts, Mahoney relied on the witness testimony and requested that Gen. Douglas MacArthur's staff locate the commanding officer of Kwajalein at the time of the reported executions.

Unlike Rear Adm. Monzo Akiyama, who had replaced Vice Adm. Koso Abe as Kwajalein commander in November 1943, Abe was very much alive. He was found in Japan and was arrested and placed in Sugamo Prison. On March 2, 1946, Lieutenant Mahoney, translator Lt. David Osborne, naval investigator Cdr. John Murphy, and court reporter Yfc. William A. Bell, all of whom had flown to Tokyo for the interrogation, met the prisoner.[12]

Lt. David Osborne was a gifted linguist. He was a graduate of the U.S Navy's Japanese Language School in Boulder,
Colorado, and had served as a translator with the Marines in
several Pacific battles.[13] Osborne had Mahoney's full confi-
dence. Armed with Osborne's skill and his own experience
dealing with Japanese prisoners, Mahoney proceed to grill
Admiral Abe.

Although Mahoney states in his unpublished memoirs that
the Marshallese natives told him of an execution in the fall of
1942, the testimony of Lejana Lekot on the execution of American fliers seems to be the evidence that Mahoney used to question Abe:

> I, LEJANA, Marshallese Native, was a laborer on
> Kwajalein Island during the month of January 1943. It
> was during this month that nine American fliers were
> brought to Kwajalein in the early part of the month on a
> Japanese ship. The fliers came from Maloelap. I talked
> with two of the nine fliers. At about 10 o'clock one morn-
> ing in January, all nine fliers were taken in a truck to the
> end of the Island. The Japanese dug holes and placed lum-
> ber over the holes. The American fliers were blindfolded
> and hands were tied. They were ordered to kneel down on
> the lumber. The Japanese then talked with the fliers and
> chopped off their heads with a sword. About forty Japa-
> nese were present. One Japanese swung the sword. The
> fliers were then buried. I witnessed the execution and the
> burial of the fliers. I could recognize the Japanese that
> swung the sword if I saw him again. Rear Admiral Abe
> was the Japanese Commander of Kwajalein at the time.[14]

Two hours into the interrogation, Mahoney had made little
progress, and with his eighty-sixth question of Admiral Abe,
the lieutenant banked on Abe's ignorance of American law.[15]

Mahoney told Abe that he had witness testimony that a Japanese unit on Kwajalein beheaded nine American fliers early in 1943 or about that time. He then told Abe that if he persisted in lying he would be charged with perjury. According to Mahoney, tears welled up in the guilty admiral's eyes. Abe confessed that he knew of the execution; however, it was not fliers who had been killed, but rather prisoners who were taken during the Makin battle. Abe went on to say the he had intended to ship the prisoners to Japan until a staff officer from Tokyo, Lt. Cdr. Sadatomo Okada, informed him that a ship could not be diverted to Kwajalein and that the prisoners were to be disposed of on the spot. In accordance with what he viewed to be Japanese policy, Abe stated, "I disposed of the prisoners there."[16]

Abe provided the date of the execution as October 1942 and insisted that no execution had taken place in January 1943. Beyond this he gave no details of the execution other than the fact the he "believed" the men were beheaded. The admiral did provide Mahoney with the name of the guard unit commander, Capt. Yoshio Obara, and of Capt. Koichi Hiyashi, Abe's senior staff officer who presided over the execution.[17]

Although Lieutenant Mahoney's team tried to keep the interrogation a secret, the following morning's Tokyo edition of the *Stars and Stripes* featured the headline "Marine Atrocity Uncovered." Lieutenant Mahoney feared that tracking down Abe's officers would now be impossible.

Upon returning to his office Mahoney found that Koichi Hiyashi was waiting to turn himself in. Claiming he had learned of the investigation by reading the *Stars and Stripes* that morning, Hiyashi identified himself as the former executive officer on Kwajalein who had directed the Marines' execution as per the guidance of Admiral Abe. Hiyashi had prepared a written statement and a diagram of the execution.[18]

The newly confessed murderer made one request of Mahoney. Hiyashi claimed that all of his family, except for his two daughters, had died in the bombing raids, and he wanted to see his daughters before his incarceration. Mahoney was shocked at the request and reminded Hiyashi of his war criminal status. Feeling that Hiyashi had proved his honor and because Hiyashi had not yet been arrested, Mahoney allowed Hiyashi a week to return home and visit his daughters. Hiyashi returned a week later for his transfer to Guam for the trials scheduled there.[19]

Before the new prisoners were transferred to Guam on the USS *Topeka*, Capt. Yoshio Obara, the guard unit commander, was interrogated in Tokyo. In his interrogation, Obara gave the date of the Marines' arrival on Kwajalein as September 2, 1942. Obara claimed that his men were on very good terms with the prisoners and got along with them very well. In a statement taken a day after his interrogation, Obara claimed that his men and the Raiders talked about Japanese customs and Japanese women. The Raiders, according to Obara, looked forward with great impatience to sightseeing in Tokyo. The Japanese captors gave the Raiders sweets and candies. In fact, because the Raiders could not use chopsticks, they were accommodated with rice balls. They were even given free medical care for several cases of diarrhea.[20]

Despite this comradeship between the prisoners and their captors, while on the veranda of Admiral Abe's quarters one evening, Captain Obara was given the order to execute the nine Marines. Because the Marines had been in Obara's charge for forty or fifty days, he claimed he was surprised by the order. Obara told the interrogators that he had suggested to the admiral that the execution would be a violation of international law, but Abe did not concede.

The execution was not carried out until five or six days

after the order, on October 16, the day of the Yasukuni Shrine Festival. Obara claimed that this date was chosen to honor the souls of those executed. In an additional show of the "relationship" the guards had with the prisoners, Obara claims that no one volunteered to execute the Marines.[21] Still, executioners were found, and the execution took place at eleven o'clock in the morning on the southwest end of Kwajalein. Obara described the spot as a twenty- to thirty-meter clearing surrounded by coconut groves.

A hole was dug in the center of the clearing, and mats were placed around the hole. The prisoners were kept waiting fifty meters from the hole. They were brought out one at a time with blindfolds on and were made to squat on the mats. The beheadings lasted about thirty minutes and were carried out singly with a Japanese sword. Obara stated that sailors stood by with pistols to spare the prisoners suffering "in case the beheading was not done skillfully."[22]

Obara did not leave out his "feelings" concerning the Raiders' execution. He testified that he felt as though he had been freed from a heavy burden after the execution, and he went back to his unit and drank whiskey.

Captain Obara's interrogation was not the last time the Raiders' execution was described. In May 1946 Adm. Koso Abe was tried in Guam under the Navy War Crimes of the Pacific program under the direction of Adm. John Murphy. The trial began with the opening statements of prosecutor Lt. Edward L. Field. Lieutenant Field had earned his law degree before the war but was not originally assigned to the war crimes trials. However, after being overheard debating aspects of war criminal prosecution by senior officers on Kwajalein, Field found himself on the prosecution team in the trial of Koso Abe.[23]

Field's opening statement accused Admiral Abe, Captain

Obara, and Obara's executive officer, Lt. Cdr. Hisakichi Naiki, of being present at the execution of the nine Marines who had been "left stranded on Makin." The three were also accused of seeing that the Marines' executions were carried out.[24] Although Abe had not denied being present at the execution during his interrogation, he had left the impression he was not present.

Capt. Koichi Hiyashi's testimony cleared up any doubts as to Admiral Abe's whereabouts during the beheadings. According to Hiyashi, he and Admiral Abe arrived on the scene in a black automobile just prior to the second execution. The senior officers stayed for several minutes and left after the second execution. According to Hiyashi, the condemned men were brought out to the pit one at a time, and he saw only one prisoner while at the site. Lieutenant Commander Naiki, who was in charge of the execution site, also confirmed that Abe was at the execution. Naiki stated the he and Obara had been present the night before the execution when the holes were dug. Naiki followed the prisoners to the execution site and ensured all preparations were made.

According to Naiki, before the executions began he went to the execution waiting room and then walked around the jungle, checking the guard posts. Because he had become "good friends" with the prisoners, he did not want them to be executed nor did he wish to see the murders. Naiki claims that when he returned to the waiting room it was empty and the prisoners had been executed.

Like Captain Obara, Naiki claimed that the prisoners had been treated well while they were on Kwajalein. Lieutenant Commander Naiki says that he housed prisoners in the last barracks, which were in the rear of his men's barracks. The executive officer testified to giving the Marines the same food his men ate and to allowing them baths and clean clothes whenever they requested them.

Forty-nine-year-old Lejana Lekot was the only Marshallese witness who testified at the trial. Whether or not Lekot witnessed the executions of fliers on Kwajalein is unknown. Given his statement to naval investigators after the war about fliers from Maloelap, which is consistent with the missing airmen's point of departure, it seems he did witness some flier executions. However, in the Abe trial Lekot testified that the Raiders' execution was the only one he witnessed.

While Lekot's and other native statements are confusing, it is clear that Lekot's testimony refers to the Raiders' execution. Lekot testified that because he was a cook for Abe he was warned about the execution before it occurred. On the day of the execution he was asked to take a table to the execution site. Curious, Lekot decided to hide behind some bushes and see what happened. As he watched he saw a truck pull up and off-load the nine Americans, who were blindfolded with their hands tied behind their backs. The truck was not the only vehicle that Lekot saw. He also described seeing Admiral Abe's black car arrive on the scene. The execution of the first marine was more than Lekot could handle, and he left shortly after witnessing the murder.[25]

By the time Admiral Abe testified on May 18, 1946, his memory had been "refreshed," and he too remembered being at the execution. While Abe had been originally unwilling to confess, during his trial testimony he admitted his guilt and displayed it in an unrepentant fashion. In fact, he went so far as to admit that he knew that the Raiders' execution was against international law.[26]

In the prosecution's closing argument, Field stressed the horror of the act that took place on Kwajalein: "In the middle of October 1942, a small clearing in a tropical grove on the southwest end of Kwajalein was converted into a bloody charnel as the heads of nine American Marines rolled in the dirt in accord with the cruel and sadistic lust of the defendants now in this court."[27]

Lieutenant Field also made it clear that the prosecution knew that Captain Obara had executed the first Raider. Lieutenant Commander Naiki's attempts to whitewash his role were also revealed. According to Lieutenant Field, Naiki's chicanery was not sustained, and it was clear to the prosecution that Naiki was present for the executions. Naiki himself admitted to greeting Abe, who did not arrive until the first execution was over.

The prosecution succeeded in its mission, and some justice was meted out for the nine Americans' needless deaths. Captain Obara and Lieutenant Commander Naiki did not escape the court's reach. Obara received a ten-year prison sentence and Naiki received four years.[28] Obara served only half of his sentence and was released on December 27, 1951, from the Sugamo Prison in Tokyo. Naiki was released on March 3, 1950, from Sugamo, after having served four years.[29] Former Vice Adm. Koso Abe, however, was sentenced to death for the nine Raiders' murders and was executed by hanging on June 10, 1947.[30]

Chapter Six

PACIFIC HEROES

War crimes trial testimony portrays the Japanese on Kwajalein as the Raiders' chummy and benevolent captors. The accused Japanese depicted themselves as hosts displaying *kantai* (hospitality) to the Marine prisoners.[1] They painted a picture of a Japanese and American island utopia that lasted right up until the dreadful but "honorable" beheadings. While this utopia has historically been accepted as fact,[2] a further examination of the accused's and American POWs' testimony reveals a different story.

Adm. Koso Abe and Capt. Koichi Hiyashi were the unrepentant exceptions to the long list of war crimes defendants hoping for leniency. Hiyashi not only turned himself in but also gave the most consistent and believable testimony. Those who twisted the truth in attempts to secure leniency—namely, Captain Obara and Lieutenant Commander Naiki—fueled the false perception that the Raiders were kept in a hotel-like prison as amusing guests.

As previously noted, if his fellow officers' testimony is to be believed, Naiki lied when he claimed not to have witnessed the left-behind Raiders' executions.[3] Captain Obara, who claimed in his testimony to have agonized over the Raiders' execution, was actually named by the prosecution as one of the men who swung the sword. Still, from the testimony of these men, the widely accepted history of the Raiders' good treatment was derived.

Louis Zamperini was most likely the first American to learn of the Raiders' execution and the only man to see a list of the names of the nine men. His experiences not only give insight into the life of an American POW trapped on Kwajalein but were also directly related to the nine Marine Raiders' imprisonment and execution.

On May 27, 1943, First Lieutenant Zamperini and nine other B-24 crew members took off on an attempted rescue mission from Kualoa Air Base on Oahu, Hawaii. Their cannibalized B-24, which had been stripped of parts for other planes in the squadron, lost its engines and crashed into the ocean north of Palmyra Island.[4]

In an affidavit given to a U.S intelligence agent upon Zamperini's return to the United States, Zamperini outlined his amazing and harrowing journey.[5] Zamperini and two other crew members, Lt. Russell A. Phillips and S. Sgt. Francis McNamara, were the only men who survived the crash. Staff Sergeant McNamara eventually died of starvation several days after the crash.

After spending forty-seven days on a life raft, fighting off hunger, sharks, the elements, and the strafing of Japanese bombers, First Lieutenant Zamperini and Lieutenant Phillips were picked up by a Japanese boat on July 14, 1943. Zamperini recalls that the Japanese men on the boat wielded pistols and swords and looked as though they were scared to death of the two starved men.[6]

The boat took the two men to Wotje, where Zamperini's Japanese interrogator warned him, "Tomorrow a ship will take you to another island. We cannot guarantee your life after you leave here." This warning soon proved to be an understatement.

Almost a year after the nine Marine Raiders' arrival, the two B-24 lieutenants arrived blindfolded on Kwajalein Island. The men were rolled onto a steel landing barge and then taken by truck to their cells. First Lieutenant Zamperini, who had been a college track star and a participant in the 1936 Berlin Olympics, was by this time a starved and exhausted eighty-pound skeleton.

Zamperini was thrown into a six-foot-by-thirty-inch cell with a six-foot ceiling. The cell's small locked door led to a hallway, and little light entered the cell. The floor was wooden and had gravel and dirt on it. According to Zamperini, the first thing his eyes focused on were some crudely engraved words on the cell wall: "Nine Marines marooned on Makin Island—August 18, 1942." The nine Marines' names were inscribed on the wall under the heading, and Zamperini spent the next forty-three days memorizing these names and contemplating the Raiders' fate and his own.

Zamperini's account of this wall inscription is contrary to the charitable custody arrangement Captain Obara and Lieutenant Commander Naiki described. It is consistent, however, with the testimony of the Marshallese witness, Lejana Lekot. Lekot testified that the Raiders were originally held in the rear of the barracks and were moved shortly thereafter: "I could see in it but that was the place they were put in when they first came there, then they were gone from there and I don't know where they were taken to."[7]

Lekot's testimony is consistent with that of recently interviewed Marshall Islanders who witnessed the Raiders in captivity. According to Mr. Nixon Braind, the Japanese did not allow the Marshallese to go near the jail where the Raiders were kept.[8]

Although Americans, such as Zamperini, who were known to have been held on Kwajalein after the Raiders were most likely held under the command of Admiral Akiyama, Zamperini's testimony concerning his accommodations on Kwajalein provides a clue to the treatment of the Raiders under Admiral Abe.

Soon after Zamperini arrived on the island, a Marshallese native was allowed into Zamperini's cell. By this time Zamperini was thousands of miles from home and forty-plus days from his unit. The native stunned him with the question, "Are you Louis Zamperini of the USC Trojans?" The Marshall Islander was apparently a sports fan and had known Zamperini's name from the Olympics. After talking sports for some time, Zamperini pointed to the names on the wall and asked what happened to the nine Marines listed. The islander moved his hand across his neck to signify beheading. Samurai sword–wielding executioners had decapitated all of the Marines. The islander left Zamperini with the words, "That is what happens to all prisoners who come to Kwajalein." Zamperini's captors reinforced this fact daily, by slicing their hands against their necks and mimicking the sound of a beheading. The overwhelming affirmations of certain death weighed on Zamperini.

In addition to living with the knowledge of his impending execution, Zamperini had to deal with angry Japanese submarine crews who were based out of Kwajalein. When these men, fresh from fighting the American enemy, returned to the island, they spent their days taunting and abusing the caged airmen. While the Japanese guards could not stomach the smell of the box Zamperini was living in, the submariners' joy in tormenting the POWs overrode their disgust.

The morning after one particularly heavy day of abuse by

the submariners, Zamperini was brought into a room full of naval officers for interrogation. The officers laughed at Zamperini and his blood-caked face and asked for information on the Hawaii airfields. One of the naval officers was a graduate of a California university, and he took especially great pleasure in taunting Zamperini.

Like Zamperini, the Raiders had faced Japanese interrogation. During the 1946 trial of Adm. Koso Abe, Captain Hiyashi was asked about his encounters with the Raiders on Kwajalein. According to Hiyashi, he saw the men only once before their execution, at an interrogation. Hiyashi testified that he was seeking information from the Raiders on the system of American submarine landings and the training of American forces. Hiyashi claimed that two Japanese men who had visited America and spoke English well helped him translate during the interrogation.

In addition to the Japanese guards' constant harassment and the interrogators' psychological games, Zamperini and Phillips had to deal with living in a tropical dungeon. Blankets were not allowed in the cells, and a hole in the floor with a can served as the latrine. Because the cell was so small, Zamperini was forced to sleep with his head near the hole. Zamperini was given three rice balls a day for food. Zamperini's crewmate Phillips said the "filth [in his own cell] was indescribable."[9]

Zamperini's dysentery was so severe that he could not sit still for more than five minutes. His can was filled with blood and mucus. Maggots covered the floor, and the cell was filled with clouds of flies and mosquitoes. Zamperini's only protection came from a Japanese guard who said he was a Christian. The Christian guard tried to keep the more vicious guards away from Zamperini's cell and was able to sneak candy to him.

Along with goodwill, water was sparse in the Kwajalein cells. Several times when Zamperini crawled to a hole in the door and asked for water, boiling water was thrown on his face. Having never bathed or shaved while on the island, Zamperini had grown his beard down to his chest. He became so thin that his bones protruded though his skin, and it was impossible for him to be comfortable in any position.

Despite the atrocious conditions and the visible signs of Zamperini's impending death, he was given no medical treatment. The closest thing he received to medical attention were the experiments the Japanese conducted on his body. Zamperini and Phillips were taken out into the prison yard and were injected, in front of a hundred Japanese personnel, with enough coconut juice to cause them to break out in rashes. Their experiences with Japanese science were not uncommon to other prisoners of the Japanese.[10]

One day Zamperini's captors informed him that his execution date was set. Contracting dengue fever turned out to be an answer to his prayers. The illness made his pain more bearable and the fear of execution more tolerable. As the day of his execution drew nearer, his thoughts were directed to those nine Marines who had preceded him.

It was a lonely existence. I looked up at the names of the nine Marines who were executed, but now I considered them my cell mates. I took a name each day and wondered about the person's life. I asked myself, "What did he look like?" And "Where was he from?" "Did he have a girlfriend, or was he married?" "Did he have children?" "How would his family take the news of his death?" I wondered about his fearful reaction or last emotional thoughts as the sword came swiftly down, sending his head rolling. Was he buried on the island, or taken out to sea? This was all I had, these 9 names of devoted Marines and heroes of the Pacific. Soon I would be joining them.[11]

Because a Japanese naval officer suggested that Zamperini's famous name could be useful in propaganda broadcasts, Zamperini and Phillips were not executed. Instead they were put on board a "hell ship," where the torment continued until they reached Japan, at which time it increased again until Zamperini's release after the war.

Zamperini and Phillips were not the only survivors of Kwajalein who told stories of maltreatment. Of the three missing B-24 crews later executed on Kwajalein, two crewmen survived their time on the island and the war. According to a sworn statement by Capt. Fred F. Garrett to a Navy war crimes investigator, he, Lt. Col. Arthur J. Walker, and their crew were shot down off Maloelap Atoll, Marshall Islands, in December 1943.[12] A Japanese boat picked up the two men and five other crew members. The Japanese on the boat repeatedly beat Captain Garrett's broken ankle and wounded leg until they landed on Millie Atoll. Lieutenant Colonel Walker and Captain Garrett were then separated from the crew and flown to Kwajalein.

As was the case with the Raiders and Zamperini, high-ranking Japanese naval officers interrogated Garrett. He was told that if he didn't talk he would not be given medical attention. Garrett was thrown into a ten-by-four-foot cell. Like Zamperini's room, it had a filthy hole for a toilet. According to Garrett, his ankle became infected, and he was forced to use his dirty trousers as a bandage. As a result, flies from the toilet laid eggs that hatched into maggots in the open wound of his ankle.

Captain Garrett and Lieutenant Colonel Walker were not alone on the island. Frank Tinker, a Marine Corps pilot whose A-24 crashed off Jaluit on December 23, 1943, was taken to Kwajalein by boat. Tinker, who helped Garrett by nursing his leg, remembers trying to communicate with other Americans in the prison by passing notes under the walls. According to Tinker as many as twenty-one Americans and a patrol bomber crew were in the prison at one time.[13]

On December 22, 1943, Garrett was told that his ankle would be cut off. On December 27 he was taken outside and left in the sun for three hours. Japanese hospital patients struck him and burned him with cigarettes. Garrett was then taken into the hospital and tied to a bed: "When I protested and wanted my leg cut off below the knee the Japanese doctor made me understand that I was a pilot and that he would cut off my leg where if I lived, I could not fly a bomber again. I was given a spinal anesthetic and was forced to watch the amputation."[14] The doctor performed a careless amputation.

Garrett was thrown on the back of a truck two days after his surgery and then flown to Truk Atoll and eventually to Ofuna Prison Camp in Japan. Frank Tinker and Lieutenant Colonel Walker made the flight with Captain Garrett. The night before the flight, Japanese officers had been forced to hold off, with pistols, angry Japanese enlisted men. The men had wanted to kill the Americans.

Captain Garrett was one of the few "lucky" ones to survive Kwajalein. The toll of Americans executed on Kwajalein is not known. In addition to Lieutenant Colonel Walker's crew, two other B-24 crews were seen last on Kwajalein. In fact, Marshallese statements give evidence that American executions on the island were not out of the ordinary.

Despite the Japanese naval officers' manipulation of the truth, we now know for certain that American POWs on Kwajalein were mistreated. The Raiders were most likely treated similarly to those who came after them. The war in the Pacific brought Americans face to face with a foreign enemy with foreign ways. Not only did the Japanese look different than most Americans, they lived and fought differently. More important to the unfortunate men who were captured by them, the Japanese had a different set of ethical standards in their treatment of war prisoners. In most cases their standards were based little on ethics and more on their sense of "honorable" murder.

The significant disappearance of American servicemen in the Pacific from 1942 to 1944 is no surprise given the Japanese's growing fear and resentment of the fast-approaching reach of the American forces. The Americans' raids and bombs turned Japanese-held atolls and islands into Pacific bomb shelters and guard posts. Boredom and relaxation were no longer options, and the threat of death increased with each day. American POWs were tangible targets for Japanese anger and fear. They had little hope of surviving the wrath of undersupported and desperate far-flung commands.

What makes the stories of Americans who died on Kwajalein amazing is the courage and the difficulty of the missions and orders they followed that resulted in their executions. They died for freedom, and their efforts led to eventual victory in the Pacific. Still, they died in circumstances unknown to their families and country.

Books, memorials, records, and stories of surviving prisoners of war and veterans tell of the unique heroism demonstrated by the men who died in the Pacific theater. These men overcame, despite limited training and support and occasionally flawed leadership, much danger, and they fought a merciless enemy who exhibited no shame in killing prisoners and later in hiding the truth.

Chapter Seven

CARLSON AND ROOSEVELT AFTER THE RAID

Following the Makin raid, Carlson and Roosevelt led the Second Battalion Marine Raiders to much success against the Japanese in the fall of 1942 at Guadalcanal. In March 1943, a reorganization of the Raider units began, and Lt. Col. Alan Shapley replaced Carlson as the Second Raider Battalion commander. Shapley was a more orthodox Marine and believed that Carlson's Makin raid was a "fiasco."[1] Under a new commander, the Second Marine Raider Battalion fought in the Solomon Islands again at Bougainville but was disbanded along with the other Raider units in early 1944.

Carlson did not command again, and he eventually served as the Fourth Marine Division's operations officer. In this position, he participated in the Tarawa, Kwajalein, and Saipan invasions.[2] Roosevelt briefly served as the commander for the Fourth Battalion Marine Raiders before he was replaced by a more traditional Marine officer, Lt Col. Michael S. Currin.[3]

The leaders of the celebrated Makin raid both left the Marines at the rank of brigadier general. After the war, Carlson continued to speak out on political issues. Histories cite that Carlson began a run for the U.S. Senate but dropped out because of his failing health. He died in 1949.

Controversy and charges of Communism continued to follow Carlson even after his death. The most interesting charge came from an unlikely source. In a 1972 interview, James Roosevelt claimed that Carlson ran for the U.S. Senate as an official candidate of the Communist Party. Dr. Charles Grossman, the personal physician of General Carlson at the time of his death and the director of the Evans F. Carlson Friends of the People's Republic of China, publicly disagreed with Roosevelt's claim. Dr. Grossman said that some Democrats in Southern California wanted Carlson to run for the Senate but that he had a heart attack and decided not to. "He was never a communist and he never ran as a communist. People have said all kinds of things about him that have been wrong."[4]

The California State Archives has no record of Carlson as a U.S. Senate candidate. Former California attorney general Robert Kenny, like Grossman, recalls that Carlson had considered running for Senate as a Democrat, not a Communist:

> The problem came into focus over the question of a candidate to run for the U.S. Senate. For a while I thought we had a solution in the person of Col. Evans Carlson of Carlson's Raiders. He was revered by the Left, and the Right was awed by his political mystique. But Carlson was a dying man, and by January he knew it and withdrew his name. My next happy inspiration was James Roosevelt, who had served under Carlson. But he declined to run.[5]

Roosevelt disputed the idea that Carlson was a choice for the Democrat ticket: "He was married to a lady who was frankly and openly a member of the communist party. As soon as this became known (and it became known that his political views were not very different from hers) the whole idea of his becoming a Democratic candidate never was seriously considered by anybody."[6]

Roosevelt, who rejoined private business after the war, became the Democratic Party chairman and ran unsuccessfully for California governor in 1950. He was later elected to the House of Representatives, where he served for nine years. He died in 1991.[7]

Chapter Eight

THE SEARCH FOR THE FORGOTTEN RAIDERS

Given the controversy that has surrounded the raid, Gen. Evans F. Carlson, the missing Raiders, and any historical comment on the subject, this chapter attempts to answer the inevitable furtherance of debate to come by providing the research background for the footnotes of this work. It also expounds on what has happened since the Raiders were left behind; their story did not end with World War II. The results of a year-and-a-half-long investigation into the whereabouts of the missing Raiders' remains are the foundation for this entire book.

The successful Makin recovery mission in 1999 brought hope that a Kwajalein recovery was possible as well. Following the Makin recovery, the sort of attention Ben Carson had been trying to garner for the cause of recovering the missing Raiders was finally developing. In the spirit of their commitment to their comrades, World War II's Marines did not forget their missing brothers. On August 17, 2000, fifty-eight years after the day the Makin raid began, the National Marine Corps League, at its convention in New Orleans, Louisiana, unanimously passed a resolution, to be forwarded to the Senate Select Committee on POW/MIA Affairs, requesting that the following be secured from the Japanese government:

- The identification, by name, of the nine U.S. Marine Raiders who were beheaded
- The disposition and location of the nine Marines' burial site
- Apologies for the inhumane atrocity to the next of kin, the Unites States, and the U.S. Marine Corps
- The nine Marines' remains, for honored burial by the next of kin and/or the U.S. government

In September 2000 I began my first day of a new job as a historian/analyst for the U.S. Army Central Identification Lab–Hawaii (CILHI). CILHI is now the Joint POW/MIA Accounting Command (JPAC), a joint service unit commanded by a flag officer. When I started working there, CILHI was an Army unit commanded by a colonel and divided into four major components: Command and Support, Search and Recovery Operations, Casualty Data Analysis, and the laboratory.

CILHI was the field-operating element of the Casualty Memorial Affairs Operations Center under the Adjutant General of the Army, U.S. Army Personnel Command. CILHI was located, as JPAC is today, on the back end of Hickam Air Force Base in Honolulu, Hawaii. It conducted investigation and recovery operations all over the world, from Vietnam to North Korea to Germany to Papua New Guniea, and had a threefold mission:

1. Search for, recover, and identify remains of American military personnel, certain American civilian personnel, and certain allied personnel unaccounted for from World War

II, the Korean War, the Vietnam War, and other conflicts and contingencies; and search for, recover, and identify related records

2. Conduct humanitarian missions and operations for emergency support as directed

3. Provide technical assistance in humanitarian and emergency operations as requested by the appropriate geographic commander in chief (CINC)[1]

At the time I began my employment with CILHI, the lab had recently completed a successful recovery of nineteen Raiders' remains from Makin Island, and CILHI anthropologists and dentists were in the process of identifying them. I viewed with awe the fallen patriots' remains on the lab tables during my first visit to CILHI. I also saw knives, a helmet, and other artifacts brought back from the recovery. I had read some background on the raid, but I had little working knowledge of the raid and the missing Raiders.

As a historian/analyst I was assigned to the Casualty Data Section, which was CILHI's analytical cell. The Casualty Data Section was headed by Rick Houston, a former Graves Registration soldier and a Vietnam veteran. Mr. Houston assigned me the job of finding out where on Kwajalein Island the nine abandoned Raiders had been executed and buried. He also gave me the time, assets, encouragement, and support to accomplish the task of conducting a historical investigation into the whereabouts of the executed Raiders' remains.

The Casualty Data Section was a locked windowless room filled with rolling shelves of military records and surrounded by cubicles for casualty data analysts. Casualty data analysts were all civilian Department of the Army employees, and each was assigned to a different conflict (Vietnam, Korea, World War II, and the Cold War). Most World War II POW/MIA research conducted at CILHI's Casualty Data Section relied on the individual deceased personnel files of MIAs, missing aircrew reports filed by the Army Air Corps, battle reports and medical records, and any other available war records.

The search for the missing Raiders posed a unique problem. At the time of the raid, no one thought these men had been left alive; it had been assumed they were dead before the unit left the island. I knew that finding someone with firsthand knowledge of the men's unintentional abandonment would be tough.

CILHI's materials on the missing Raiders consisted of a letter from Raider Ben Carson, excerpts from a war crimes trial, and a small published book about the Raiders. I realized early on that to find the detailed answers to the question of the missing Raiders' whereabouts I would have to search out any and all sources related to Lt. Col. Evans F. Carlson and his Raiders and Makin and Kwajalein islands. During my search I obtained or attempted to obtain anything and everything on these subjects from veterans, archives, libraries, and the Internet. I also continually reminded myself that the answer was out there somewhere.

With the hope that the answer lay in war crimes testimony or long ago boxed-away trial exhibits, I began my search by calling Japanese war crimes trial historians. Unfortunately, the trials held in Guam were the least studied and written about. The trials in the Philippines and Tokyo had been the focus of the war-era media and later historians, and in fact, I could not find a single history that focused exclusively on the Guam trials.

Robert Barr Smith, a retired Army colonel and a law professor at the University of Oklahoma, directed me to the papers of Adm. John D. Murphy, head of the War Crimes Commission in Guam, which are now archived at the Hoover Institution at Stanford University. Barr also mentioned that the Naval Historical Center had a copy of the *Final Report of Navy War*

Crimes Program. But Barr believed that Murphy's papers would hold what we were looking for.

Through an Internet search of the National Archives' modern military history holdings database, I was able to find a listing of copies of the war crimes trials held at the National Archives in College Park, Maryland. National Archives archivist Rich Boylan and Defense Prisoner of War/Missing Personnel Office (DPMO) historian Dr. Jean Mansavage generously offered to search the archives for the war crimes trials. DPMO is the Defense Department office responsible for the oversight of policies on the rescue of Americans who are isolated, captured, detained, or otherwise missing in a hostile environment and the recovery of those who don't return from foreign battlefields.[2]

Mr. Boylan and Dr. Mansavage quickly produced a copy of the Koso Abe's war crimes trial in Guam from the archives and sent the proceedings to Hawaii. Both the National Archives and DPMO continued to lend valuable assistance to CILHI throughout the investigation.

The war crimes proceedings contained a good deal of information relevant to the investigation. One exhibit included a sketched map of the execution site, which, according to testimony, was also where the Raiders were buried. The execution and burial site appeared to be inside the turn of a road. The trial proceedings did not provide, however, the specific geographic details needed to pinpoint the burial site. Testimony indicated only that the area was on the southwest end of the island.

Kwajalein Island is now inhabited strictly by Americans, many of whom are interested in World War II and Kwajalein history. In the years since the execution, well-intentioned citizens have proposed countless theories as to where on the island the Raiders were killed. Many of these theories were sent to CILHI and each was checked out, but none of these theories seemed plausible and all placed the site outside of the road. The proceedings of the war crimes trials helped to debunk these well-meaning but historically inaccurate theories.

As a quick study on the raid and armed with new information on the Raiders' fate, I decided to start calling Raider veterans. I realized the veterans could not provide me with much firsthand information on the missing Raiders' fate because the Raiders had been presumed dead by all men on the raid when the battalion left the island. I did, however, hope to get a good idea of what happened during the raid and what led to the abandonment of the nine men. Additionally, I realized that the veterans would be the ones to know any new information that might have come to light in the years since the raid. Finally, and most important, I hoped these men could provide clues as to who, out of the twelve unaccounted for Marines, the nine left-behind Raiders were.

I spoke with several Raiders and learned early on that the Raider veterans were divided in their views of Carlson and all were spirited in their opinions of their leader. General Carlson had a strong and loyal following. Through the years his name had become synonymous with the Raiders, and because of this, many Raiders who either were not on the raid or who served after the Makin raid have a strong loyalty to him and are very protective of his name. Some Raiders believe, however, that the raid did not go as planned and that Carlson's leadership was questionable. One such lighting rod for this opinion is Second Marine Raider Ben Carson. Carson has not stopped seeking answers since he first learned the Raiders were missing. He has continued to ask hard questions in his quest for the truth when many would like to forget history.

Carson provided me with a firsthand account of the raid and of his continuing efforts to find and recover the missing servicemen's remains. Mr. Carson was able to give me a detailed account of the raid, those involved, and the names of the missing who were possibly killed prior to the nine Raiders' beheadings. He was also up front about the controversies surrounding the raid, its leader, and the missing Raiders. Through Carson I was able to speak with other Raiders about the raid and their take on what happened.

Phone conversations and correspondence with historians who had written about either General Carlson or the raid proved very helpful. Historian Phyllis Zimmerman passed along Raider Charles Lamb's report on the raid discussed in chapter 3. Lt. Col. Jon T. Hoffman, author of *From Makin to Bougainville: Marine Raiders in the Pacific War* and a historian at the Marine Corps Historical Center in Washington, D.C., provided me with the location information for the original Makin raid operation reports at the archives. All of theses sources buoyed Ben Carson's firsthand account. In fact, everything Carson told me during the investigation was backed up by every primary source revealed during the investigation.

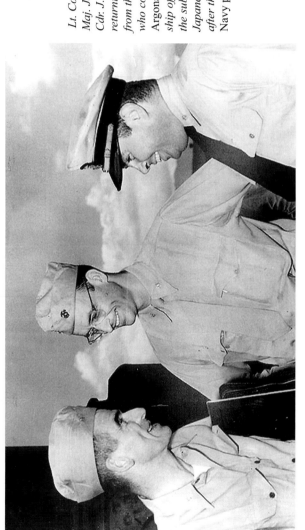

Lt. Col. Evans F. Carlson, Maj. James Roosevelt, and Lt. Cdr. J. R. Pierce upon returning to Pearl Harbor from the Makin Raid. Pierce, who commanded the USS Argonaut, went down with his ship off of New Britain, where the sub was destroyed by Japanese shells, five months after the Makin Raid. Official Navy photo

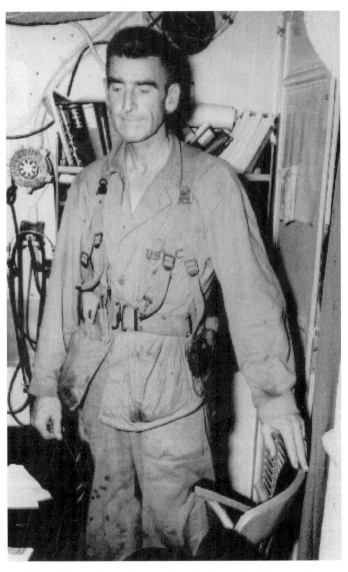

Lt. Col. Evans F. Carlson on board the USS Nautilus *shortly after the raid.* Official Navy photo

Admiral Kamada surrenders the Marshall Islands (September 10, 1945). Interpreter, Tech Sgt. Don Okubo (center) had previously landed on Airik Island (Admiral Kamada's headquarters) alone and demanded to see the admiral; at that time he secured a promised surrender from Kamada. Okubo was awarded the silver star for his actions. Photo from the Military Intelligence Veterans Club of Hawaii's fiftieth anniversary book, M.I.S. Personnel, World War II Pacific Theater (1993); courtesy of Albert Koyanagi and Don Okubo

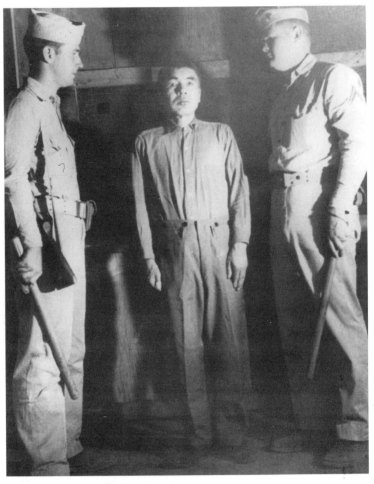

Former Vice Adm. Koso Abe at the war crimes trials on Guam. Abe was hanged for the execution of the Raiders. National Archives photo; found at Richard Flores Taitano Micronesian Area Research Center

Former Kwajalein POW Louis Zamperini, in Tokyo after the war with a former Japanese naval officer who presumably helped spare Zamperini's and crew member Russell A. Phillips's lives by suggesting to fellow officers that the men should not be executed but should be sent to Tokyo and used for propaganda. Zamperini met with many of his former captors while on a Billy Graham crusade in Japan. Zamperini is the only man known to have seen the names of the nine missing Raiders on a Kwajalein prison wall and live to tell about it. Photo courtesy of Lou Zamperini

Lt. Col. Arthur J. Walker's B-24 crew. The crew was taken prisoner by the Japanese and is believed to have been executed on Kwajalein. Only Lieutenant Colonel Walker (standing center) and Capt. Fred F. Garrett (not pictured) were not killed. Walker and Garrett were separated from the crew and eventually flown to Japan, where they both survived the war. Photo turned over to U.S. naval investigators by surrendering Japanese admiral Kamada

Crew of the B-24 Baby Sandy II, taken prisoner by the Japanese and believed to have been executed on Kwajalein. Virgil Tramelli is the first man in the first row. Photo turned over to U.S. naval investigators by surrendering Japanese admiral Kamada

The eleven missing Raiders following the Makin Raid.

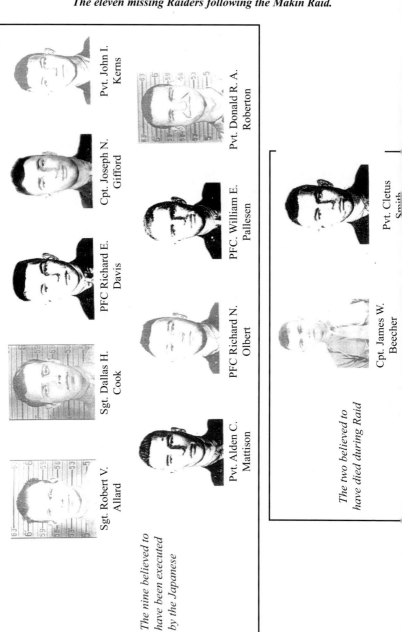

Pvt. John I. Kerns

Cpt. Joseph N. Gifford

PFC Richard E. Davis

Sgt. Dallas H. Cook

Sgt. Robert V. Allard

Pvt. Donald R. A. Roberton

PFC. William E. Pallesen

PFC Richard N. Olbert

Pvt. Alden C. Mattison

The nine believed to have been executed by the Japanese

Pvt. Cletus Smith

Cpt. James W. Beecher

The two believed to have died during Raid

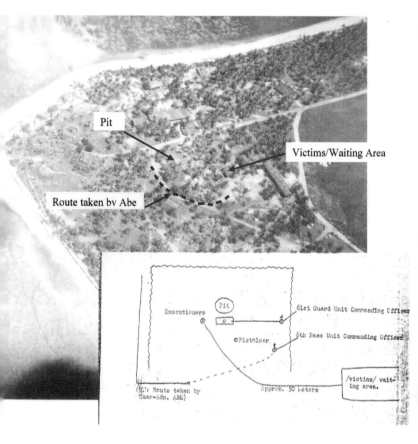

Sketch drawn by Admiral Abe's staff officer who presided over the execution, Koichi Hiyashi. The former Japanese captain provided the sketch and the most reliable information to the U.S. naval investigators regarding the executions. The photo is of the southwest end of Kwajalein island and the area of the execution. The map was drawn by Hiyashi several years after the war for his memoirs. Sketch courtesy of the National Archives; official Navy photo

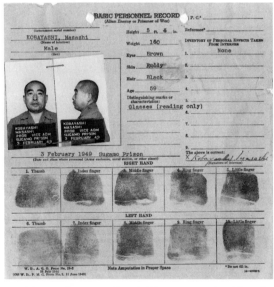

The incarcerated former Japanese Fourth Fleet commander, Masashi Kobayashi. The former admiral admitted to being given an automobile tour of the Raiders' burial site by Adm. Koso Abe. American servicemen who survived the prisons of the Fourth Fleet, such as Lou Zamperini, testified to the horrible conditions and lack of food there. In contrast, notice the appearance of Kobayashi after three years in an American prison (second photo). National Archives photo

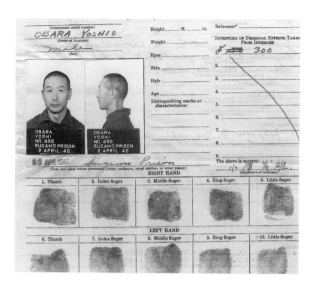

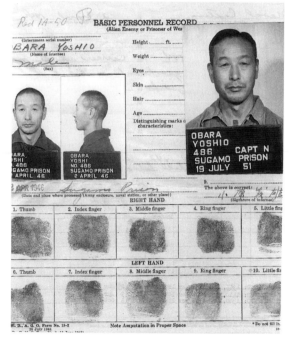

The incarcerated former Kwajalein Guard Unit commander Yoshio/ Yoshi Obara. Obara executed the first Raider. He served four years of a ten-year prison sentence. National Archives photo

(Alien Enemy or Prisoner of War)

NAIKI, HISAKICHI
(Interment serial number)
(Name of Internee)
(Sex)

Height......ft.......in.
Weight.................
Eyes...................
Skin...................
Hair...................
Age....................
Distinguishing marks or characteristics:

Reference* 25 MAR '46

INVENTORY OF PERSONAL EFFECTS TAKEN FROM INTERNEE

1.
2.
3.
4.
5.
6.
7.
8.
9.

The above is correct:
(Signature of Internee)

NAIKI,
HISAKICHI
NO.758
SUGAMO PRISON
20 APRIL 46

20 APR 1946
(Date and place where processed (Army enclosure, naval station, or other place))

RIGHT HAND

1. Thumb	2. Index finger	3. Middle finger	4. Ring finger	5. Little finger

LEFT HAND

6. Thumb	7. Index finger	8. Middle finger	9. Ring finger	10. Little finger

Like Obara's, former Japanese lieutenant commader Hisakichi Naiki's false testimony in the Guam war crimes trials has perpetuated the myth that the Raiders were treated well on Kwajalein before their deaths. Naiki was in charge of the execution site and served a four-year prison sentence for his role in the Raiders' deaths. National Archives photo

Ambassador William P. Mahoney (formerly Lieutenant Mahoney, USN) with President Kennedy. Mahoney, a judge adjutant general officer, was the U.S. naval investigator who discovered the execution of the Raiders and built the case against Admiral Abe and others involved in the execution. Photo courtesy of Ms. Eileen Mahoney

Ben Carson (far left) and Louis Zamperini (far right) on Kwajalein for the CILHI recovery mission. A Kwajalein Public Affairs officer is next to Carson and archaeologist Karl Kuttriff is next to Zamperini. Photo courtesy of Ben Carson

The author (left) with Menke Kanel (center), a Marshallese Islander who saw the nine Raiders as POWs on Kwajalein. Marshallese interpreter Noda Lojkar is on the right. Photo courtesy of Tripp Wiles

The "controversial" plaque (above) that was dedicated on Kwajalein on Memorial Day 2002. The plaque was removed because of the words "left behind" and was replaced with another (below) on Veterans Day 2003. Photo courtesy of Jack Miller

Chapter Nine

A SEARCH THROUGH HISTORY

Four months after the CILHI investigation into the Makin raid began, in January 2001, I was sent by CILHI on a research trip to the Hoover Institution in Stanford, California; the National Archives at College Park, Maryland; the Naval Historical Center and the Marine Corps Historical Center at the Navy Yard in Washington, D.C.; the Army's Center for Military History at Fort McNair in Washington, D.C.; and finally the Air Force Historical Research Agency at Maxwell Air Force Base in Montgomery, Alabama.

My first stop was the Hoover Institution, home of the Murphy Collection. The collection consisted of several boxes of war crimes trial proceedings, which yielded additional testimony on the executed Marines' burial, in a copy of Admiral Kobayashi's trial proceedings. This was perhaps the most helpful find for the Kwajalein investigation.

The proceedings revealed that while visiting Kwajalein, Admiral Kobayashi, who was the Fourth Fleet commander, was given an automobile tour of the executed Americans' gravesite by none other than Adm. Koso Abe. The former Imperial Japanese Navy admiral also mentioned, by name, the Kwajalein buildings they passed on the way to the site. This testimony validated a CILHI theory that the site was very near a road.

Admiral Kobayashi also testified that while in a Guam stockade in 1948, a U.S. Marine guard showed him a sketch of the execution burial site. This bit of information led to many questions, including, Who was the guard and is he still alive? Which sketch was prisoner Kobayahsi shown?

Also among the Murphy papers were POW statements to war crimes investigators concerning the mistreatment they received at the hands of the Japanese on Kwajalein. Louis Zamperini was one of these men. Mr. Zamperini later played a crucial role in the investigation.

Shortly before I left for my research trip, I received a package from the Naval Historical Center in Washington, D.C. The package contained the microfilm copy of the *Final Report of Navy War Crimes Program*. I took the box with me in hopes of viewing the film on the trip. While at Stanford, I found an open microfilm machine and viewed the film.

As I sat in the Stanford University library I was angered and horrified by what I read. I viewed, through poorly microfilmed records, crimes of absolute power gone mad. I knew that the Japanese military had done awful things to Allied POWs and the natives of countries they conquered, but to see actual accounts of murder, cannibalism, rape, and torture roll before my eyes was another story. I scrolled through atrocity after atrocity, with only the names of the islands and Japanese captors changing in each account; the brutal acts against unknown victims were the same. The phrases "American beheaded" or "native killed" were too numerous too count.

The end of the film showed the eerie black-and-white photos of the accused and the Judge Advocate General counsel with, thanks to poor microfilm technology, unwittingly blacked-out faces. The final pictures showed the condemned and the executed. I left the library that evening with a renewed sense of purpose. I wanted to know what really happened to the Raiders.

The next leg of my research trip was spent mostly at the National Archives in College Park, Maryland. The archives contained Makin raid operational reports and preinvasion maps. The collection also held Carlson's after-action report and the scathing after-action reports and comments by Carlson's counterparts and superiors.

The after-action reports provided further confirmation of the command and control issues that Ben Carson had spoken with me about. These reports clearly differed greatly from the accounts of the raid by the popular media at the time and even today. The fog of war and groundbreaking warfare operations notwithstanding, something had gone terribly wrong on the raid, something that in turn led to nine Raiders being left behind.

The archives' cartography section contained a preinvasion map of Kwajalein that correlated somewhat with Kobayashi's testimony and CILHI's general theory on the grave location.

The staff at the Marine Corps Historical Center produced what to me was a rare find: a copy of George Noran's journal. Noran's journal gave firsthand testimony of the Raiders' first days marooned on Makin, before they were captured by the Japanese. The journal also provided the identity (Takanu, the Makin Islander) of the set of remains found buried among the nineteen Raiders during CILHI's Makin recovery mission.[1]

Unfortunately the Naval Historical Center did not have additional exhibits or documents belonging to the war crimes collection. The Navy's war crimes records collection had been forwarded to the National Archives many years before, and this was in fact the collection that we had already viewed and copied at the archives.

The last portion of the trip was to Maxwell Air Force Base. The Kwajalein-related information I viewed in their archives consisted of blueprints for the northeastern end of the island after the war.

When we returned to Hawaii the investigation took a new turn. As I read the proceedings over and over, several questions arose: Did U.S. naval investigators, interpreters, and Judge Adjutant General officers associated with the 1946–48 Guam war crimes trials know exactly were the burial site had been? Was the burial site even a concern at the time? Were any of these men involved with the trials alive?

I began to consider the names on the pages potential living witnesses. The names of translator David Osborne, judge advocate Lt. Edward L. Field, judge advocate and war crimes investigator William P. Mahoney, and Yfc. William A. Bell appeared throughout the war crimes investigation testimony and the trial proceedings. If the burial location was known at the time of the trials, these men would know about it.

I did not know where to begin in my search for these veterans. I had no idea where they were from, where they went after the war, or what profession they chose. I began by calling the Navy and the Veterans Administration (VA). I assumed that, if the men had retired, the Navy or the VA would have their addresses for mailing retirement checks. Neither of these institutions had any record of these men retiring.

I considered trying to obtain the men's personnel records from the National Personnel Records Center at St. Louis, but unfortunately, as I had discovered early in my employment at CILHI, our status as a military organization searching for POWs and MIAs afforded us no special privileges in ordering the personnel records. We at CILHI, just as thousands of others who endure the arduous process of ordering and waiting for files, started at the back of the line. The clock was ticking and I did not have time to wait for the files, so I began searches on the Internet. This became my primary means of finding many of the hard-to-locate veterans I interviewed for this investigation.

After several Internet searches, I found the phone number for the Osborne residence. Mrs. Osborne informed me that her husband had recently passed away. We spoke for a while, and she told me about his life after the war, including how he had been a wonderful man and had gone on to become the U.S. ambassador to Burma. Unfortunately for the CILHI investigation, Mr. Osborne did not leave any papers from the war crimes investigations.

Through Ben Carson, I was also able to find William P. Mahoney's family. In a conversation with Mahoney's daughter, I learned that, like his counterpart, he had recently died. He had also gone on after the war to serve as a U.S. ambassador. When I asked if her father had left behind any documents that might be useful to the investigation, Mahoney's daughter generously offered to forward me an unpublished copy of her father's memoir.

Unfortunately the name William A. Bell proved to be too common, and I had no luck finding him. This was especially unfortunate because (if his rank was any indication) he may have been the youngest of the men involved with the trials.

In May 2001, after several phone calls, I discovered that the lead prosecutor of Admiral Abe's trial, Edward Field, was still living. I placed a call to Mr. Field, who remembered being involved in the trials but did not have a great recollection of the Admiral Abe trial. Mr. Field asked me to send him copies of the trial materials. Mr. Field's opening statement in the trial had been a stirring tribute to the men killed by the Japanese on Kwajalein, and it was my hope that his powerful oration would trigger his memory of the trial and the surrounding investigation that supported the proceedings.

After viewing the war crimes trial proceedings, Mr. Field said that he started to remember bits and pieces of the trial. He told me that the investigators had not been worried about where the graves were but were strictly concerned with prosecuting the war criminals. According to Mr. Field, he could not recollect where exactly the execution/burial site was on the island, but he vaguely recalled that the graves were at the end of the runway and that at the time of the trials the airstrip was being extended, requiring a lot of construction. According to Mr. Field, he finished his duty at the trials in September 1946.

With a stall in progress on the war crimes trial front, a new door opened in the investigation. One afternoon Rick Houston asked me to speak with a man from St. Louis named Jim Tramelli. According to Mr. Houston, Mr. Tramelli claimed his uncle, a World War II Army Air Corps pilot, was a POW who was executed in the Marshall Islands by the Japanese. He believed his uncle was executed on Kwajalein. Unsure of the validity of his story, I called Mr. Tramelli. Mr. Tramelli explained to me that with our assistance, a few months before, he had obtained a copy of the individual deceased personnel file (293 file) of his uncle, 2nd Lt. Virgil Tramelli. Individual deceased personnel files, for all intents and purposes, are owned by the Army, regardless of the deceased's branch of service. These files are held at the National Records Center, a National Archives–administered records repository in Suitland, Maryland. Since the 293 was the foundation for CILHI World War II POW/MIA research, CILHI was continually ordering these files; they were shipped to Hawaii on a weekly basis. The Casualty Data Section was itself becoming somewhat of a repository for these files. What free space was available in the office was being filled with stacks of boxes filled with 293 files.

Each branch of service has a Service Casualty Office that is tasked with assisting the family members of the missing and killed in action. Often when a POW/MIA's family member calls the Service Casualty Office for assistance, the Service Casualty Office has to defer to CILHI because we now hold so many files. These 293 files contain anything and everything known about the missing or deceased individual, including his or her last-known whereabouts, a missing aircrew report if a plane was involved, and reports of any searches for the individual. The file holds letters to the military from family members and letters to the family from the military. Copies of some medical and dental records and inventories of the serviceman's belongings that were left behind in the barracks are included. The 293 files are in most cases a historical reminder that the military tried in earnest to find America's missing.

The execution of Army Air Corps bomber crewmen on Kwajalein was news to us at CILHI. Unfortunately, it was news to the Tramelli family as well. Upon receiving a copy of his uncle's 293, Mr. Tramelli and his family were shocked to find in the file a photo of Virgil Tramelli and some of his fellow crew members in what appeared to be a POW camp somewhere in the Pacific. The men in uniform were holding up placards with Japanese writing on them. The crew members' names were written on the back of the photo. The Tramellis were surprised because the last time they had heard from the government, they were told that Tramelli was missing in action and presumed dead. They had heard rumors of a capture but never from the U.S. government. For almost sixty years, Jim's father, John, Virgil's younger brother by eleven years, had believed that Virgil had died in a plane crash. No one in the family had any idea that he had died a prisoner of war.

While speaking with Mr. Tramelli on the phone, I walked over to the boxes of 293 files. Thumbing though World War II–era manila files I came across 2nd Lt. Virgil Tramelli's name and service number. Opening the file I flipped through the old carbon copy and browned pages directly to the photo, and I too was shocked at what I saw.

Mr. Tramelli was not angry, but he was definitely disappointed in his government. Like most POW families, though, he was grateful that someone, after all these years, was interested in helping his family find some answers. Jim Tramelli's call led us in CILHI to realize that the Raiders might not have been the only Americans executed on the island.

Jim Tramelli had heard stories about his uncle all his life, and he looked up to him a great deal. Virgil Tramelli had been a merchant marine before the war and had also spent time as an actor for the St. Louis Municipal Opera. Below is an excerpt from a letter from 2nd Lt. Virgil Tramelli to his family shortly before his death. The letter became a reminder to me of why CILHI continued to search for answers.

Dear Mom, John and to my dear ones at home,
I somehow feel it a strong obligation to set down briefly a few thoughts which would be apropos in the event of my death. The reality of my part in this war is here. I have been a part of it for quite some time now. Already, there are those who have gone before me. I have come to realize it clearly that though we all wish to survive this war, we all cannot. For those of us who do not, there must be one consolation. It is imperative, as it is our great comfort, when we go into action, that we are a part of a great nation. That our entire history from our very beginning was a struggle for the same things which we fight for now.

It will be all of your duties to keep America great and insure her that her sons have not died in vain—in this light, ours is a man's death. I cannot ask for more.
Lovingly,
Virgil

After speaking with Jim Tramelli, I spent a good deal of time studying the files of his uncle and the missing aircrew and the history of that day in the air war. I soon learned that the prisoners' story provided great insight into the treatment the nine Raiders most likely received on Kwajalein.

In December 1943 Seventh Air Force B-24s were striking Japanese installations in the Marshall Islands in preparation for the coming U.S. invasion and Operations Flintlock and Catchpole. On December 29, 1943, the Eleventh Bomb Group, 431st Bomb Squadron B-24J 42-73013, *The Baby Sandy II*, and its crew crash-landed on a reef in the northwest end of the lagoon on Majuro Atoll, Marshall Islands, after being hit by enemy fire and losing two engines on a bombing raid from Tarawa. According to reports from other American airmen, found in the 293 file, escort aircraft tried to protect the downed aircraft; however, Japanese Zeros strafed the plane. It is not known whether pilot 1st Lt. Ivan M. Osborne and copilot 1st Lt. Raymond D. Cloyer died from wounds suffered from the crash or at the hands of the Japanese.

War crimes investigations conducted by the Navy revealed that the remaining eight crew members—1st Lt. Maxie G. Deer Jr., 2nd Lt. Virgil A. Tramelli, T. Sgt. Edward J. Bislew, Pvt. Williston F. Rumsey, S. Sgt. Hulbert J. Swaim, S. Sgt. John J. Dell, T. Sgt. Joseph J. Perry, and S. Sgt. Warren C. Hill—were taken prisoner, sent to Maloelap, and then finally shipped to Kwajalein. The crew members' files proved to be a tremendous source in the Kwajalein investigation. They also proved to be the first of many reminders that the practice of executing Americans on Kwajalein was not a one-time occurrence.

An additional source of Jim Tramelli's belief that his uncle was executed on Kwajalein was found in the 293 file in the form of a report from an American Graves Registration Service (AGRS) team who had visited the Marshall Islands in 1949.

While on Kwajalein the team spoke with a local named "Bien." Bien was an employee of the Island Trading Company and was on a ship that brought what he referred to as "the eight Americans" to Kwajalein.

According to Bien, the ship was bombed on its way to Kwajalein, but none of the men were hurt in the bombing. The Americans were off-loaded onto Kwajalein, and Bien never saw them again. Bien believed that the men were questioned and then executed, "which seemed to be the Japanese Practice at time."[2]

The report went on to say that the team had questioned Bien and other locals about the location of American gravesites on Kwajalein, "but all stated that the American bombing of Kwajalein destroyed all markers and so churned up the ground that there was no chance of finding it now."[3] This, in my opinion, was an obvious red flag for the CILHI investigation.

After hearing the story of Tramelli's crew, viewing the witness statements, and realizing how small Kwajalein was, it was my hope and theory that all Americans who were executed on Kwajalein were buried at a single site. If this proved to be the case and CILHI was able to find the Raiders' execution/burial site, then our chances of finding more than the Raiders' remains were greater. The burial site was a concern for the scientific staff at CILHI as well, and the archaeologists felt that, if in fact the Raiders' graves or any mass American burial site had been bombed, there would still be human remains in the soil.

The natives' comments about the site, though, understandably concerned me. I wondered if the investigation might be stopped before an excavation was begun. Dr. Mansavage had been searching the archives for any Marshall Island American Graves Registration records in the hope that, if any unknown remains were found on Kwajalein after the American invasion, they might be those of the POWs we were looking for. Although

I had come across the words "Kwajalein unknowns" in a 293 file, we could not find any other mention of Kwajalein unknowns in any of the records during the entire investigation.

As I continued to read through the 293 file, I found investigation reports from shortly after the war that showed evidence that an additional bomber crew went down in the area and that several crew members were missing. One confidential extract reported that other bomber crews were lost in the area and mentioned the capture of Zamperini and Phillips. The report also stated that an Admiral Kamada had submitted the "photographs" of 2nd Lt. Tramelli's crew and Lieutenant Colonel Walker's crew. This was the same Admiral Kamada who, when he surrendered, told naval investigators the common lie that all U.S. POWs on his island had died when U.S. planes bombed the Japanese ships on which they were being transported to Kwajalein.

The rest of Virgil Tramelli's 293 file made it clear to me that after the war the U.S. investigators were unsure of how many Americans had survived their plane crashes only to be later killed on Kwajalein by the Japanese. Sixty years later we at CILHI were in the same boat.

The investigation appeared to be yielding some fruit. The many contacts I had made through phone calls and e-mail were beginning to produce results. When the memoir of former war crimes investigator William Mahoney arrived in the mail at CILHI, he further confirmed that bomber crews were missing in the Marshall Islands. His memoir also provided great insight into the missing Raiders' last days and how the war crimes investigator discovered that the Raiders had been executed.

One of the most interesting finds happened on Oahu at the Bishop Museum. One day, after being cooped up in the office researching, I decided to go to the museum to see if they had any holdings related to the Marshall Islands. I was hoping for photographs of Kwajalein, but I had no expectations.

When the curator asked me what I was looking for, I mentioned that I was interested in World War II–era photos from the Pacific theater. To my surprise, the curator said that he had thousands of World War II aerial photographs of Pacific islands. According to the archivist, in the 1960s the Joint Intelligence Command Pacific (JICPAC) had thrown away aerial photographs of Pacific islands. A JICPAC employee, who also worked at the Bishop Museum, scooped up the photos and took them to the museum.

After going though hundreds of photos, I found exactly what I was looking for: a 1944 pre–Kwajalein invasion close-up photo of the southwest end of the island. This photo proved to be an invaluable tool of the investigation.

Another extremely helpful tidbit came from DPMO in Arlington, Virginia. While I was conducting the investigation from Hawaii, DPMO's Dr. Jean Mansavage continued to search the National Archives for any information on Marshall Islands war crimes trials and investigations. Thanks to Dr. Mansavage's research, a bulk load of Marshall Islands war crimes investigation documents arrived at CILHI. The documents were filled with new names and avenues of research.

These investigation records were essentially the information used by the war crimes prosecutors as evidence for the first war crimes trials in the Marshall Islands. Among the records was an interview of a former Japanese guard who had been on a boat that ferried American POWs to Kwajalein. The guard remembered that one of the prisoners had been an actor before the war. 2nd Lt. Virgil Tramelli's nephew had told us that his uncle had been an actor before the war; the guard must have been referencing Tramelli's crew.

The records also provided the names of the missing aircrew headed by Lieutenant Colonel Walker and the names of additional missing bomber crew members. The records enabled

CILHI to order the crew members' 293 files. Sure enough the files of Lieutenant Colonel Walker and his crew contained a photo similar to the Tramelli crew photo.

The 293 files revealed that, as with the rest of the Seventh Air Force B-24s, Lieutenant Colonel Walker's crew in December 1943 was pounding enemy installations in the Marshall Islands in preparation for the coming invasion. Lieutenant Colonel Walker's crew went down just days before Tramelli's crew was lost.

On December 15, 1943, on a bombing mission from Nanumea, Ellice Islands, against Maloelap Atoll, Marshall Islands, B-24J 42-72969 of the Thirtieth Bomb Group, Twenty-seventh Bomb Squadron was damaged by antiaircraft fire and crashed into the sea twenty miles northeast of Taroa Island, Maloelap Atoll. Engineer T. Sgt. John D. Travers, assistant engineer S. Sgt. John R. Ormesesher, and assistant radio operator Lester G. Shwam were believed to have died of wounds some time after the crash. A passenger on the plane, Maj. Thomas F. Harper Jr., died ten hours after the crash while on a life raft and is believed to have been buried at sea.

A Japanese ship, the *Susho Maru*, picked up Lt. Col. Arthur J. Walker and six other surviving crew members—T. Sgt. Virgil F. Abbott, 1st Lt. Fred F. Garrett, 2nd Lt. Charles W. Holland, S. Sgt. George S. Lunsford, 2nd Lt. James Palladino, and 2nd Lt. Donald E. Wright—from a life raft. The Japanese photograph turned over to the United States after the war shows six of the crew members after their capture. First Lieutenant Garrett is not pictured, most likely because of his wounds. On December 19, 1943, Lieutenant Colonel Walker and First Lieutenant Garrett were separated from the rest of the crew and were flown to Kwajalein, where the Japanese amputated First Lieutenant Garrett's leg. Thankfully Lieutenant Colonel Walker and First Lieutenant Garrett survived the war. (I was unable to find and contact either of these men.) Unfortunately war crimes investigators concluded that the five other crewmen were taken to Kwajalein on December 23, 1943, and were never heard from again.

The third missing bomber crew was the last of the three missing bomber crews CILHI was now aware of. According to the 293 files, on January 3, 1944, B-24D tail number 42-42105 took off from Tarawa on a bombing mission to Taroa Island, Maloelap Atoll. The B-24 was hit over Wotje and forced to make a beach landing on Arno Atoll. Two of the ten crew members—gunner S. Sgt. Henry R. Wyka Jr. and engineer Sgt. Marion L. Farmer—were killed in the crash, and their bodies were later recovered.

According to a statement in the missing aircrew report, the remaining eight crew members—pilot 1st Lt. Roger W. Morse, copilot 1st Lt. Herbert S. Evans, navigator 2nd Lt. Robert H. Wirostek, bombardier 2nd Lt. William F. Carpen, assistant engineer and gunner S. Sgt. L. L. Stowe, radio operator T. Sgt. John W. Horman, radio operator and gunner Pvt. Robert P. McTwigan, and gunner S. Sgt. Paul H. Vanbuskirk—were housed and fed by natives on Arno from January 3, 1944, until January 16, 1944, when a Japanese patrol landed from a boat and captured the crew. The crew was tortured, and the Japanese killed several natives. According to the statement, one officer had a broken shoulder and another had a broken leg from the crash. The crew was taken to Majuro and then to Kwajalein, where they were most likely executed.

An additional document found in the file was an interpreter's report on U.S. Navy base letterhead. It tells a slightly different version of the incident. The report states that five Japanese occupied Arno at the time of the crash, and one of these was a Japanese policeman named Masunaga. According to the report, the policeman sent some deputies to investigate the incident. After it was reported that ten Americans and two men were wounded, the policeman sent out the natives to capture the American airmen. The report goes on to say that the Americans were captured without a struggle and that the Japanese policemen took their watches and rings and placed them in solitary confinement. The report reveals that one American died the next day at "7 o'clock" and that an American plane flew over Arno in search of the missing. The report also details how a storekeeper's feeding of the Americans angered the Japanese. The report states that eight Americans were taken on January 15, 1943, on a Japanese ship. Last, the report explains that one American was found dead on the beach and that the natives buried him with the other American in the cemetery, even though the Japanese told them not to do so.

Because several executions took place on Kwajalein Island, witness statements collected by investigators often acted as helpful but confusing aids to the investigation. The circumstances surrounding the missing aircrews and the investigation reports that were filed provide numerous examples of the problem faced by the war crimes investigators at the time and CILHI sixty years later. Each bomb crew had a similar number of men, and the crews were lost within a short time frame. Additionally, as I was beginning to learn, the Japanese had every reason to lie about what had actually happened. This only made things more confusing at the time and compounded the historical challenges CILHI faced. As a result of these conflicting statements, it was sometimes impossible to determine to whom witnesses were referring.

For instance, the story of eight captured men forwarded to Kwajalein on a ship that was sunk by a U.S. aerial attack appeared, in several variations, in several war crimes investigation records of Japanese officers' testimony. After seeing the story over and over and comparing it to the testimony of a Marshallese witness who stated that his ship was in an attack but the men survived, it was clear that in at least one instance, the Japanese were trying to avoid blame for the execution of Americans on Kwajalein.

Throughout the war crimes investigation records I saw the name Nathan G. Finkelstein. After locating Finkelstein's phone number I optimistically called his home. A family member mentioned that Finkelstein had been sick and could not come to the phone but that he knew about the war crimes investigations. When I asked if I could send him a package of records, I was told that he was moving to Florida soon and I was given his address and phone number there. After sending the records, I attempted to follow up by phone twice, but I was met with unwelcoming responses and was never allowed to speak with the man who had been so involved in the investigation of missing Americans in the Marshall Islands.

A phone call to World War II veteran and former POW Lou Zamperini was a refreshing jump start to my research. Zamperini greatly enhanced the investigation and offered an amazing story and further clarity to the stories that had already been recounted in the investigation. Mr. Zamperini related his harrowing experiences on Kwajalein as a POW, including his discovery of the names of the nine Raiders on his cell wall. During several phone calls, Mr. Zamperini related information that opened up numerous avenues of research and what I perceived as possibilities of finding the answers we were searching for.

Mr. Zamperini suggested that I call former Marine Corps pilot and POW Frank Tinker. Mr. Tinker was more than happy to speak with me and to help the investigation. Mr. Tinker further validated my growing belief that several American MIAs were executed on Kwajalein, and he also shed new light on Lieutenant Colonel Walker and his crew. Mr. Tinker brought a surprisingly new revelation to the table when he related that several U.S. Navy POWs were likely killed on the island as well.

Mr. Tinker told me that he took off in an A-24 from a carrier off of Makin Island on December 23, 1943. Mr. Tinker was shot down, and his gunner was killed. Tinker was captured by the Japanese and was taken to Jaluit. His Japanese captors beat him after he crashed, but after spending the day in Jaluit, he had a conversation with a Japanese officer with a good translator. Mr. Tinker then endured a bad three-day trip on a launch to Kwajalein. He was put in a cell with Lieutenant Colonel Walker and Garrett. Lieutenant Colonel Walker had a broken back, but Tinker doesn't think the injury affected the colonel aside from making walking difficult. While Mr. Tinker nursed Garrett's injured leg, the Japanese were relentless; they kept coming in and kicking Garrett's wounds.

The prisoners passed notes to each other under the walls. They believed that there were about twenty-one of them there. Mr. Tinker believes some of the POWs were Navy PBY boys (PBYs were amphibious Navy patrol planes). Tinker told me that the Japanese men were angry because of the continued bombings by the United States; they wanted to get their hands on the American prisoners. After surviving a few close calls, Tinker, Garrett, and Walker left Kwajalein on a boat for Japan. Mr. Tinker assumes the Navy POWs were executed.

The more we searched for the answers to the question of the Raiders' final fate, the more deaths we learned of, and it soon became apparent that Kwajalein had been an execution island. The nine Raiders, possibly two bomber crews and members of a third, and now several sailors appeared to have been murdered on the island.

In May 2001 the investigation took another turn. It was becoming very clear to me that the information we were looking for was not going to be easy to find and would probably come from an unlikely source found through even more extensive research. The answer might even come from Japan. Dr.

Mansavage had provided for a link to Japan through Japanese historian Hitoshi Kawano. Mr. Kawano placed an ad in a Marshall Islands veterans group publication requesting any information on the missing Raiders and quickly received a response from a veteran who had been on a ship that transported the men to Kwajalein. Unfortunately the man knew little else about the Raiders, but his response alone created hope that someone in Japan had information about the Raiders.

Time and again I requested that I be put in touch with someone to help me get in contact with someone in the government who could request cooperation from the Japanese, but time and again I met resistance. The embassy made promises that never panned out, and no one seemed to believe the Japanese government's cooperation was a possibility.

I also pressed for a way to speak with Marshallese who had been alive when the Raiders were captured and executed. I was denied this request and was told that because of the low life expectancy in the Marshall Islands, no one who could have witnessed the raid was still alive.

I refused to give up, however, and I contacted the U.S. foreign area officer for the Republic of the Marshall Islands. After several radio spots and ads, the officer reported negative results. I also called an American diver who lived in the Marshall Islands and had worked with CILHI on past recoveries. He promised to ask the locals if they knew anything about the Kwajalein investigations. The diver also told me that a group of Japanese had been traveling throughout the Pacific for several years and cremating remains of Japanese missing and killed in action. The diver feared that the Japanese might be inadvertently cremating American remains.

After checking this story out with several sources, I immediately passed the concern on to CILHI's command. Given America's track record with the Japanese government on World

War II investigations, I was doubtful we would be able to discuss these issues with the Japanese. Although the cremations would be a major problem for other Pacific investigations and recoveries, because Kwajalein had been manned by the United States since the war and because it was so small, I doubted that the group could have collected remains on Kwajalein.

I continued to pore over the photo of Kwajalein I had found at the Bishop Museum. I also used all photo computer software available to me to enhance the area. With the continued assistance of Dr. Mansavage at DPMO, CILHI was able to pass the image on to the Defense Intelligence Agency for depression analysis.

As many times as I looked at the photograph, I could not get it to match with the testimony of accused Japanese war criminals and former Imperial Japanese Navy Lt. Hisakichi Naiki. I also could not resolve the fact that, if the execution and burial site was where we believed it to be, then our theory was incompatible with the photo and Naiki's testimony. This was perplexing to me until I remembered Lou Zamperini's story of captivity.

Ever since I had begun the investigation I had read accounts from historians about how the Raiders were treated well up until their execution. According to accounts, the Raiders were kept in a building adjoining the Japanese barracks. The Japanese had joked with the Raiders and hated to see them executed. The historians' source of information had no doubt been the war crimes trial proceedings and had come straight from the accused war criminals themselves, men fighting for their lives.

Remembering Lou Zamperini's affidavit and my conversations with him helped me realize that the Raiders were not treated well. Zamperini and every other former POW who had survived Kwajalein had testified to the awful conditions they had faced. More convincing though was Lou Zamperini's account of the names carved into his cell wall. This proved that at least one of the Raiders had been in the same miserable cell that he had been in. I became convinced that Naiki's detailed story of his long walk along a jungle path and the beach during the execution did not work out on a map or aerial photo because his testimony was not true. Naiki was trying to convince the Americans that he was so attached to the Raiders that he could not bear to see them beheaded. In the process, he had hidden the truth from both the public and investigators sixty years later.

Chapter Ten

THE INTERPRETERS

With few options remaining in the search for Navy veterans, I initiated a search for Japanese American Military Intelligence Service (MIS) veterans, or Nisei, who may have been directly involved in translating for the trials or interrogating the prisoners.

I learned that a deacon in my church, Al Koyanagi, had been a Nisei interpreter on Iwo Jima. I spoke with Mr. Koyanagi about his experiences and our investigation, and he brought me a copy of a publication MIS personnel had put together for their fiftieth anniversary, titled *Secret Valor: M.I.S. Personnel, World War II, Pacific Theater, Pre-Pearl Harbor to Sept 8, 1951.* The publication contained the accounts of men who had served, and I was grateful to find included the account of Don Okubo, a U.S. Army interpreter who participated in the Marshall Islands war crimes trials.

To my surprise, after searching for Mr. Okubo's phone number on the Internet, I learned that Don Okubo was a Honolulu resident. I immediately arranged for an interview with Mr.

Okubo at his home. Mr. Okubo single-handedly brokered the surrender of Admiral Kamada, who incidentally turned over photos of two aircrews he had sent to Kwajalein. One of these aircrews included 2nd Lt. Virgil Tramelli and the other was Lieutenant Colonel Walker's crew. Perhaps the most valuable piece of information that Mr. Okubo gave me for our investigation, though, was the name and phone number for another MIS veteran, retired U.S. Army colonel Harry Fukuhara.

When I called the retired colonel, he was very amicable and interested in helping with the CILHI investigation. He mentioned that he and his brother were planning a trip to Honolulu, and while he was in town, he wanted to meet for lunch to discuss exactly what CILHI needed.

Continuing in my review of what I had already covered in the investigation, I decided to view the *Final Report of Navy War Crimes Program* microfilm. I noticed the name Eugene Kerrick near the end of the film. By now I had learned the ins and outs of searching for names, and I knew when I saw "Kerrick" that he would be easy to find. Fortunately for me, he was.

Eugene E. Kerrick was a U.S. Navy Japanese language officer. He arrived in Guam on Labor Day weekend 1946 and was involved in the trial of Vice Admiral Kobayashi. I related the story of the corporal showing Kobayahsi a sketch of the execution site, and this prompted Mr. Kerrick's memory of a Japanese-American corporal who had converted to Catholicism, making the Japanese mad. Mr. Kerrick could not remember the corporal's name but mentioned that the University of Colorado–Boulder had an archives of their language school graduates; he thought that the information in the archives or the graduates themselves might be able to help.

Mr. Kerrick also suggested that I call Mr. Calvin Dunbar, a Marine interpreter who left Guam in April 1946. Mr. Dunbar told me that he had done a lot of work on Truk and Roda. He said the Marines graduated seventeen classes of no more than ten men from Camp Ellis. The last class graduated in 1945. According to Mr. Dunbar, interpreters started out as corporals. Mr. Dunbar's information gave me some idea of the field of veterans I would be looking for.

After speaking with Messrs. Kerrick and Dunbar, I decided that every effort should be made to contact those involved in the war crimes trials who might have known the execution/burial location of the Raiders killed on Kwajalein. I believed that it was important to research all available papers of these men, living and deceased. To begin my search for the survivors of the war crimes trials and their papers, which could lead to the execution/burial site location, I traveled to the University of Colorado in Boulder.

Shortly after World War II, several of the graduates of the Japanese Language School (JLS) at the University of Colorado in Boulder were sent to Guam to assist in the investigation and prosecution of Japanese war criminals. Sixty years later the University of Colorado had begun archiving the interpreters' papers and had reestablished contact with several of these men. The JLS archives is the only repository for the papers of Japanese language interpreters involved directly with the investigation and trials of criminals responsible for the death and disappearance of American service members in the Pacific theater. It was my hope that the JLS would be able to assist CILHI in the Kwajalein case and future Pacific-area cases that involved war crimes.

While in Boulder, I looked through the files, personal papers, and correspondence of JLS graduates and graduates of the Marine Corps' Japanese language schools from around the country. One of the problems I had encountered previously in searching for the trial participants was that in many cases, only the last names were given. The archives in Boulder yielded the full names of men who worked as interpreters for the Guam war crimes trials and often their contact information. The archives also revealed names and contact information of Navy JAG officers (noninterpreters) involved in the Guam war crimes trials. The papers contained detailed lists of graduates of the Marine Corps' Japanese language schools; I hoped the lists might lead me to the corporal who assisted in Admiral Koba-yashi's trial and was referenced as having a diagram of the Marines' execution site.

The JLS archives also had contact information for Nisei historians who could possibly assist CILHI in finding Nisei participants in the Guam trials. The archives held an additional lead in newspaper clippings of the *Navy News*'s (Guam edition) coverage of the war crime trials, but none revealed the location of the execution/burial site.

While at the university, I met with the head archivist of the JLS collection, Mr. David Hayes. Mr. Hayes was in close contact with the JLS graduates and edited a monthly newsletter, *The Interpreter*, that was sent to the Navy and Marine interpreter veterans. I submitted to Mr. Hayes a CILHI request, to be published in that month's addition of the JLS newsletter, for the veterans' assistance in its Kwajalein war crimes research. I also provided Mr. Hayes with a packet that included a summary of our Kwajalein research and the areas of research concentration related to the war crimes trials. Mr. Hayes promised that he and his staff would use the packet to locate pertinent information in papers as they were submitted to the JLS archives.

After I had contacted a few interpreters, I took a break from the JLS lists and temporarily turned the investigation back to the Marshall Islands. I began to search for people who could help me track down Marshallese witnesses to the trials. The first person I found was Mr. Allen Fowlers, the general manager of the Marshall Islands phone company. Mr. Fowlers had lived in the Marshall Islands for over thirty years. He appeared to be familiar with the Marshallese individuals whose names I had extracted from the war crimes investigations, including John Iman, the interpreter for Marshallese witness Lejana Lekot, who claimed to witness the Raiders' execution. Mr. Fowlers stated that the John Iman he knew was a doctor and that he had been dead for several years. When I asked him about Bien, the Marshallese native who witnessed Americans off-loading on Kwajalein, Mr. Fowlers said the only man he knew by that name had been dead for years as well.

It was becoming apparent to me that the investigation was going to be much more difficult than I had imagined and that while finding people and documents familiar with incident was possible, finding what we were looking for might not be.

Chapter Eleven

GOOD NEWS

Frustrated by the fact that a full and thorough investigation should have taken place years before and confronted with the thought that the CILHI investigation may be too late, I went back to a report I had found in the 293 files of one of the missing bomber crewmen. I had always wanted to track down the men of the 1949 American Graves Registration search team. I had conducted numerous name searches on the Internet, but this time I was able to find what appeared to be the phone number for a diver on the team, a man who most likely had recovered several sets of remains himself from crashed bombers and fighters.

I called the phone number and was told by the diver's wife that her husband had died of cancer a few years before. The wife believed, and her husband had agreed, that the diver's cancer had been caused by his time spent diving in the Pacific near U.S. nuclear testing facilities. The wife went on to say that her husband had left some papers behind from the yearlong expedition through the Pacific, and she would be glad to forward them to me. Unfortunately the papers did not help the investigation.

In August Colonel Fukuhara and his brother arrived in Honolulu. I met them for lunch at the Army resort in Waikiki, the Hale Koa. Fukuhara and his brother listened to all I had to say about the investigation, and then they promised to help as much as they could using their contacts in the Japanese government.

After my visit with the Fukuharas, I continued to try to explore each and every potential lead. One of the leads that I had kept in the back of my mind was a document that I had found on my research trip to the National Archives in College Park, Maryland. A handwritten note from the Seventh Infantry Division, the infantry division that had invaded Kwajalein, revealed that 125 or more Korean laborers had survived the invasion. Because Kwajalein was a small island and because so many Americans seemed to have been executed there, I thought that at least one of the surviving laborers might have seen something. But I didn't know how to contact the former laborers. My best opportunity, coincidentally, arrived on CILHI's doorstep.

The South Korean military had recently begun conducting operations to recover the remains of its own fallen soldiers. A Korean TV news show was filming a documentary on this effort and also wanted to visit and film CILHI for a U.S. perspective on remains recovery operations. When I heard about this project, I knew contacting the filmmakers was the best shot I had at reaching the former labors. Thankfully, Bob Maves, a fellow analyst who would not take "no" for an answer, convinced the TV show to give me airtime. In the CILHI Korean TV interview, through an interpreter, I gave a short historical background of the Korean laborers on Kwajalein and then requested that any surviving Kwajalein Korean laborers come forward if they had information about the Raiders' burial site or anything else that would help our investigation. Unfortunately we did not receive a response, nor, we were told, did the TV station.

Through the defense attaché of the American embassy in Tokyo, I made contact with a man affiliated with several Japanese veterans group leaders. The contact had promised to help search for a Kwajalein veteran, but this lead proved to be a dead end.

While working on the Kwajalein investigation, I was also researching MIA cases in Palau. Dr. Patrick Scannon, a fine American who devotes much of his time to searching for information about POWs and MIAs, is the founder of the Bent Prop Project, a group devoted to searching for clues in the western Pacific to aid in the remains recovery of World War II POW/MIAs. Pat, in helping CILHI with its Palau investigations, interviewed a former World War II Japanese officer. The man Pat had interviewed had committed war crimes against Americans during World War II, so I knew a Japanese veteran who knew something about the Raiders' executions could be out there.

I believed that the answer to the Raiders' burial site riddle was most likely in Japan. The Japanese government's lack of interest in CILHI's Kwajalein investigation seemed to be stalling its progress. The language barrier and residual distrust from World War II greatly prohibited the success of CILHI's research in Japan.

A contact I made through the JLS veterans helped me track down some Japanese sources. Wakako Higuchi had been a Japanese newscaster and had found two Japanese books on the Guam war crimes trials. She also had contacts with Japanese Marshall Islands veterans and offered to give CILHI their phone numbers in hopes of finding a Kwajalein veteran. Higuichi believed veterans conducted Marshall Islands reunions and that they might be available for interviews.

At the time of the Kwajalein investigation, I was finishing my master's degree at Hawaii Pacific University. One of my classmates, Susumu Kato, was a Japanese foreign national, and one afternoon he readily agreed to assist me in calling Japanese war veterans. We stood at a pay phone in a downtown Honolulu department store for a couple of hours calling Japanese veteran groups to no avail.

Just when I felt CILHI might be running out of options in its search for answers from Japan, Colonel Fukuhara was able, within a few weeks of our meeting, to secure through his Japanese contacts a copy of a sketch of the Raiders' execution and burial site. Former Imperial Japanese Navy captain Koichi Hiyashi had drawn the sketch for his memoir. (Interestingly enough, a few days after Fukuhara submitted the sketch, I received a copy of the same sketch from Wakako Higuchi.)

This sketch provided a much more detailed geographic location than any previous sketches or descriptions and was the turning point in the historical investigation. The sketch confirmed that the site was on the northern portion of an area within the curve of the main Japanese road on the southwestern end of the island. The sketch, coupled with DPMO's analysis of untranslated versions of the war crimes trials, which were found at the UN archives by Dr. Mansavage, gave CILHI the confirmation it needed to move forward with the remains recovery operation.

On January 8, 2002, after the successful 1999 recovery and later identification of nineteen U.S. Marines interred on Makin Island, the U.S. Army Central Identification Laboratory, Hawaii, in an attempt to recover the remains of the nine Marine Raiders from Kwajalein Island, the Republic of the Marshall Islands, launched a mission to Kwajalein. Capt. Nathan Chamberlain headed the team, and archeologist Dr. Greg Fox was appointed to lead the recovery. Lab director Dr. Tom Holland had placed Dr. Fox in charge of the potential recovery operation early in the investigation, so Fox was very familiar with the historical investigation I had been conducting. Throughout the investigation, Dr. Fox and I discussed CILHI's theory on the execution/burial site location.

From the start of the recovery operation, several factors, seen and unseen, were working against the team. Most evident was the mixed coral and sand ground composition, similar to concrete, on Kwajalein. The team worked tirelessly in the hot Pacific sun with shovels and jackhammers to break up the ground and at the same time preserve the site's integrity. For weeks, with blistered hands, little rest, and few results, the team continued its backbreaking work. During this time, National Geographic filmed a documentary on the Makin Island raid and the left-behind Raiders entitled *Riddles of the Dead: Execution Island*.[1] A large portion of the documentary was shot on Kwajalein. The film company brought Ben Carson and Lou Zamperini to the island to witness the recovery operation.

By February a large section of the island's western end had been excavated and only a few bone fragments had been recovered. At this point Dr. Fox and consulting archeologist Dr. Carl Kuttruff deduced that the current maps of Kwajalein inaccurately displayed the location of the Japanese road that was used until the 1944 U.S. invasion. Fox decided to extend the excavation site to the north to compensate for inaccurate cartography.

Since the Raiders' burial in 1942, the heavy bombardment preceding the 1944 U.S. invasion, the U.S. cleanup, severe storms in the 1950s, and the island's manmade extension over the years had greatly affected the appearance and composition of the island's western end. Because of these changes Kwajalein lacked permanent geographical landmarks, and this compounded the challenges the CILHI team faced. The blasting of coral heads by the U.S. Navy in the 1980s additionally hampered attempts to use coral heads depicted in war-era aerial photography of the island as landmark references.

During the recovery mission, I received orders to visit Kwajalein, consult with the CILHI archeologists on site, and work to find any additional information that might help the recovery. This was not my first visit to Kwajalein. In November 2001 Dr. Fox, Captain Chamberlain, and I had visited the island and the future dig site.

While in Kwajalein in November, I took a ferry to Ebeye in the hopes of finding elderly Marshallese who knew about the executions. Ebeye is a short distance from Kwajalein and is one of the most overpopulated areas on Earth. Ebeye is home to several Marshallese who work on Kwajalein for the U.S. Army and their families. My interpreters on the island and I had failed to find a witness during the November 2001 trip, so when I received orders to go to Kwajalein in January 2002, I was determined to return to Ebeye and find a witness.

With the invaluable assistance of U.S. Army Kwajalein Atoll host nations officer Stephen Notarianni and Marshallese interpreter Noda Lojkar, I was able to speak with Marshallese citizens who had knowledge of American executions. The two men escorted me by boat to Ebeye Island and to our first visit at the home of Menke Kanel. Mr. Kanel was born in 1923 on Ujae Atoll. He had witnessed nine men off-loaded from a boat onto Kwajalein Island about a year before "the war," that is, the February 1944 U.S. invasion of Kwajalein. Mr. Kanel at first thought the men were old because he had never seen white men and had never seen young men with light hair. According to Mr. Kanel, the men were wearing military uniforms. Mr. Kanel believed that these men were from a submarine from Makin.

Mr. Kanel did not witness the execution of any Americans. His friend, Fountain Inok, however, was on the digging detail for the execution of nine Americans. According to the friend, the Japanese dug a hole, lined nine men up, shot them, and watched the men fall over into the ditch. Mr. Kanel heard that these men were killed at the end of the island. When Lojkar asked Mr. Kanel where the men were executed, Mr. Kanel, who is now blind, indicated that the site was on the island's western edge.

Mr. Kanel left Kwajalein a week before the U.S. invasion. He heard that some U.S. pilots were taken to Kwajalein Island from Jaluit by the Japanese during the war. Mr. Kanel suggested that Mr. Inok, a Marshallese worker on the digging detail, might still be alive and have information for us. Unfortunately, Mr. Inok had died a few years before CILHI began its investigation. Mr. Notarianni called Mr. Inok's son, who owns a hotel on Ebeye. The younger Mr. Inok had no knowledge of the executions or burials and had never heard his father speak of them.

It is very likely that the men Mr. Kanel saw off-loaded were the Raiders. Mr. Kanel's statement about nine men shot on the end of the island, however, was most likely a reference to MIA U.S. Army air crewmen. Marshallese and Japanese testimony makes it clear that the Raiders were beheaded, not shot. Further, the area pinpointed by Mr. Kanel as the execution site was different from the area identified by Koichi Hiyashi in his 1964 memoir. The nine men Mr. Kanel referred to were very likely U.S. aviators who were killed and buried at the end of the island in the area he indicated.

Maps revealed that much of the end of the island where Mr. Kanel claimed Americans were buried was washed away in a severe storm in the 1950s. Mr. Kanel's mention of U.S. POWs being brought to Kwajalein from Jaluit most likely is a reference to U.S. Navy TBD-1 pilots who were taken prisoner after a January 1942 air raid. These men were taken to Kwajalein and then transported to Japan.[2]

After meeting with Mr. Kanel, we met with Ato Langkio. Mr. Langkio had heard through family members that Americans had been executed on Kwajalein's western end. Mr. Langkio also mentioned that this area had been washed away by a storm in the 1950s and had later been replaced with fill.

Last we visited Anni Betwel. Mr. Betwel was born on Kwajalein in 1933. According to Mr. Betwel, a week before the U.S. invasion, he and his family were on the southwestern end of Kwajalein, where they witnessed Japanese soldiers off-load two "American pilots" in military uniform from a truck. The Americans were then beheaded. Mr. Betwel stated that the Japanese saw him witness the execution but did not care. Mr. Betwel believed that the executed Americans were members of the U.S. Navy. When Mr. Betwel was asked to pinpoint the execution site, he grabbed the map from my hand and pointed confidently and without hesitation to the same spot identified by Hiyashi as the Marine Raiders' burial site.

Mr. Kanel's and Mr. Langkio's accounts are similar to war-era U.S. Navy war crimes investigation testimony. Since it is likely that several Americans were captured and sent to die on Kwajalein under similar circumstances, it is hard to distinguish which group of men witnesses are referring to. Mr. Betwel's statements, however, further strengthened CILHI's site selection and the theory that Americans were executed and buried in the area.

In addition to the Marshellese witnesses, I spoke with several American residents on Kwajalein about our investigation. While researching the files at an office on Kwajalein, one such resident told me that a group of Japanese veterans who had served on Kwajalein during the war had visited the island in the 1980s.

The recovery team continued its work until all areas linked to historical evidence had been uncovered. The mission ended in March 2002, after much of Kwajalein's western end was excavated but yielded only small bone fragments. CILHI is currently attempting to identify the minimal remains recovered.

There are many possibilities as to what happened to the Raiders' remains. Kwajalein is a small island devastated by war and drastically changed by postwar construction. In the years after the war, what were believed to be Japanese soldiers' remains have been found. In fact, while we were on Kwajalein, Japanese remains were discovered on the other end of the island.

Some of the remains found through the years might have been those of Americans, and construction crews on Kwajalein might have mistaken American remains for Japanese. Some suggest that the Raiders' execution site is actually a few yards east of CILHI's recovery site, under a Japanese shrine and a photo lab. Without certain answers, the possibilities seem endless; we may never know the truth for sure.

At the time of this writing the U.S. Navy was building the USS *Makin Island* (LHD-8), an all-electric LHD-1 WASP-class ship.[3] The motto on the ship's crest is "Gung Ho," honoring the Raiders who died on Makin. The Raider crest is inlaid in the ship's crest to memorialize the Second Marine Raider Battalion. The inverted blue star in the crest celebrates Medal of Honor recipient Raider Staff Sergeant Thomason and a cross alludes to the twenty-three Navy Crosses awarded to the Makin Raiders.[4]

While the Raiders' courage is still being honored, regrettably the controversy over the history of the raid continues. On Memorial Day 2002 a plaque on Kwajalein was dedicated to the nine Marines executed on the island. Jack Miller, a civil servant for the Department of the Army, U.S. Army Space and Missile Defense Command, was instrumental in making the memorial to the Raiders a reality. Unfortunately, a few members of the Raider Association were so outraged that the memorial read, "the Marines were mistakenly left behind," they demanded the wording be changed. In response, a new memorial was dedicated on Veterans Day 2003. It reads, "The Marines were captured following their participation in the 17–18 August 1942 raid on Makin Island."

Although the controversy will likely continue and the whereabouts of the Raiders' remains may never be known, we know now the story of the nine American patriots who died on Kwajalein Island in defense of their country.

Appendix

RAIDERS KILLED AND MISSING IN ACTION

1. Capt. Gerald P. Holtom*
2. Sgt. Clyde Thomason*
3. Cpl. I. B. Earles*
4. Cpl. Daniel A. Gaston*
5. Cpl. Kenneth K. Kunkle*
6. Cpl. Edward Maciejewski*
7. Cpl. Harris J. Johnson*
8. Cpl. Robert B. Pearson*
9. Cpl. Mason. O. Yarbrough* (member of Peatross's platoon)
10. Field Musician Cpl. Vernon L. Castle* (member of Peatross's platoon)
11. Pfc. William A. Gallagher*
12. Pfc. Ashley W. Hicks*
13. Pfc. Kenneth M. Montgomery* (member of Peatross's platoon)
14. Pfc. Norman W. Mortensen*
15. Pfc. John E. Vandenberg*
16. Pvt. Robert B. Maulding*

17. Pvt. Franklin M. Nodland*
18. Pvt. Charles A. Selby*
19. Pvt. Carlyle O. Larson* (originally declared MIA by Raiders)
20. Cpl. James William Beecher (believed to have died in attempt to return to sub)
21. Pvt. Cletus Smith (believed to have been killed in battle)
22. Sgt. Robert V. Allard (believed to have been left behind)
23. Sgt. Dallas H. Cook (believed to have been left behind)
24. Cpl. James Gifford (believed to have been left behind)
25. Pfc. Richard E. Davis (believed to have been left behind)
26. Pfc. Richard N. Olbert (believed to have been left behind)
27. Pfc. William E. Pallesen (believed to have been left behind)
28. Pvt. John I. Kerns (believed to have been left behind)
29. Pvt. Alden C. Mattison (believed to have been left behind)
30. Pvt. Donald R. Roberton (believed to have been left behind)

---

* Individual's remains were recovered and identified by the U.S. Army Central Identification Laboratory–Hawaii (CILHI).

NOTES

Introduction

1. Michael B. Graham, *Mantle of Heroism: Tarawa and the Struggle for the Gilberts, November 1943* (Novato, CA: Presidio Press, 1993), 13.

2. *Gung Ho*, VHS, directed by Ray Enright (Universal Studios, 1943).

3. Theodore Roscoe, *United States Submarine Operations in World War II* (Annapolis: U.S. Naval Institute, 1949), 158.

4. Ibid., 157.

5. Harley Cope and Walter Karig, *Battle Submerged: Submarine Fighters of World War II* (New York: Norton, 1951).

6. Ibid., 74.

7. Samuel Eliot Morison, *History of United States Naval Operations in World War II*, vol. 4, *Coral Sea, Midway and Submarine Actions, May 1942–August 1942* (Boston: Little Brown, 1949), 235.

8. Maj. Gen. Oscar F. Peatross, *Bless 'Em All: The Marine Raiders of World War II* (Irvine, CA: ReView Publications, 1995).

9. Lt. W. S. LeFrançois, "We Mopped Up Makin," *Saturday Evening Post*, December 11, 1943, 28–48.

10. *Gung Ho*.

11. Michael Blankfort, *The Big Yankee: The Life of Carlson of the Raiders* (Boston: Little, Brown, 1947).

12. *Final Report of Navy War Crimes Program Submitted by the Director, War Crimes, U.S. Pacific Fleet to the Secretary of the Navy*, December 1, 1949, microfilm, NRS1977-57, Navy Historical Center, Washington, DC.

13. Richard Garrett, *The Raiders: The Elite Strike Forces That Altered the Course of War and History* (New York: Van Nostrand Reinhold, 1980), 184.

Chapter 1: The Raiders

1. The Gilbert Islands, along with the Line Islands and the Phoenix Islands, are now a part of the independent nation of Kiribati.

2. Adm. Chester Nimitz, "Solomon Island Campaign—Makin Island Diversion," October 20, 1942, RG 127, Records of the United States Marine Corps, Historical Files, box 183, 370-D-04-1, National Archives, College Park, MD, 1.

3. The Raider exploits were detailed in articles in the *New York Times* on August 22 and 28, 1942. A Hollywood version of the raid titled *Gung Ho*, overseen by Lieutenant Colonel Carlson, was produced in 1943. The Navy's view of the raid was presented in Theodore Roscoe's *United States Submarine Operations in World War II*. The raid is used as a background for W. E. B. Griffin's historical novel *The Corps*, book 2, *Call to Arms* (New York: Jove Books, 1987), and in Marine historian Verle E. Ludwig's *Archie Smallwood and the Marine Raiders* (Santa Barbara, CA: Daniel and Daniel, 1998).

4. Allen Reed Millett, *Semper Fidelis: The History of the United States Marine Corps* (New York: Macmillan, 1980), 234.

5. Carlson's resignation from the Marine Corps became effective on April 30, 1939. Carlson proceeded to write three books on the subjects he was not allowed to speak on while he served in the Marine Corps: *Evans F. Carlson on China at War, 1937–1941*,

ed. Hugh Deane (New York: China and U.S. Publication, 1993); *The Chinese Army: Its Organization and Military Efficiency* (New York: International Secretariat, Institute of Pacific Relations, 1940); *Twin Stars of China: A Behind the Scenes Story of China's Valiant Struggle for Existence, by a U.S. Marine Who Lived and Moved With the People* (New York: Dodd, Mead, 1940). He applied for recommission in 1941.

6. Charles Lamb, "Comments on the Raid on Makin Island Manuscript," 9, Lamb Papers, Marine Corps Research Center, Quantico, VA.

7. Phyllis Zimmerman, "The First 'Gung Ho' Marine: Evans F. Carlson of the Raiders" (unpublished manuscript, 1999), 4. Ms. Zimmerman provided a copy of the unpublished work to the author on November 2, 2000. Also, *New York Times*, August 22 and 28, 1942.

8. Zimmerman, "First 'Gung Ho' Marine," 4.

9. Ibid., 9.

10. Maj. Jon T. Hoffman, *From Makin to Bougainville: Marine Raiders in the Pacific War* (Washington, DC: Marine Corps Historical Center, 1995), 1.

11. Ibid.

12. Ibid. Also, Joel D. Thacker, "The Marine Raiders in World War II (Preliminary)," Historical Branch Assistant Chief of Staff, G-3 Headquarters, U.S. Marine Corps, 1954.

13. Hoffman, *From Makin to Bougainville*, 1–3.

14. Ibid., 1.

15. James Roosevelt, interview by Amelia R. Fry, August 10, 1972, in Amelia R. Fry, *California Democrats in the Earl Warren Era: Interviews* (Sanford, NC: Microfilming Corp of America, 1982).

16. Hoffman, *From Makin to Bougainville*, 4, 5.

17. Roosevelt interview.

18. Hoffman, *From Makin to Bougainville*, 5.

19. Kenneth McCullough, telephone interview by the author, October 25, 2000.

20. Lamb, "Comments on the Raid on Makin Island Manuscript," 4.

21. Peatross, *Bless 'Em All*, 7.

22. Roosevelt interview.

23. Lamb, "Comments on the Raid on Makin Island Manuscript," 4.

24. Zimmerman, "First 'Gung Ho' Marine," 9.

25. Denton E. Hudman, telephone interview by the author, March 17, 2003. Also, Benjamin Carson, interview by Mr. Graham, September 21, 2001, transcript, Admiral Nimitz National Museum of the Pacific War, Fredricksburg, TX.

26. Carson interview, September 21, 2001.

27. Kenneth H. Merrill, telephone interview by the author, August 13, 2005.

28. Carson interview, September 21, 2001.

29. Hoffman, *From Makin to Bougainville*, 6.

30. Ibid.

31. The task group was given the *Argonaut*, the *Nautilus*, and the *Narwhal* originally, according to Peatross in his book, *Bless 'Em All*, 46.

32. "While operating off of New Britain, the *Argonaut* intercepted a Japanese convoy returning to Rabual from Lae. After damaging one destroyer, a severe depth charge attack forced the *Argonaut* to surface and the destroyers circled and pumped shells into her bow causing her demise." Ernest M. Eller, *United States Submarine Losses: World War II* (Washington, DC: U.S. Government Printing Office, 1950), 31.

Chapter 2: The Raid

1. Lt. Col. Evans F. Carlson, "Operations on Makin, August 17–18, 1942, Written Onboard USS *Nautilus*, at Sea," August 21, 1942, RG 127, Records of the United States Marine Corps, Historical Files, box 183, 370-D-04-1, National Archives, College Park, MD, 1.

2. Peatross, *Bless 'Em All*, 66.

3. Carlson, "Operations on Makin," 1.

4. Peatross, *Bless 'Em All*, 70.

5. Ibid., 64.

6. Eleven men were lost to snipers, according to Nimitz, "Solomon Island Campaign—Makin Island Diversion."

7. R. G. Rosenquist, Col. Martin J. "Stormy" Sexton, USMC (Ret.), and Robert A. Buerlein, eds., *Our Kind of War: Illustrated Saga of the U.S. Marine Raiders of World War II* (Richmond, VA: American Historical Foundation, 1990), 40.

8. Peatross, *Bless 'Em All*, 72.

9. Donald M. Goldstein and Katherine V. Dillon, *Fading Victory: The Diary of Admiral Matome Ogaki, 1941–1945*, trans. Masataka Chihaya (Pittsburgh: University of Pittsburgh Press, 1991), 184.

10. Peatross, *Bless 'Em All*, 53.

11. Ibid., 58. See also Carlson, "Operations on Makin," 7.

12. Peatross, *Bless 'Em All*, 58.

13. W. J. Holmes, *Undersea Victory: The Influence of Submarine Operations on the War in the Pacific* (Garden City, NY: Doubleday, 1966), 165.

14. Peatross, *Bless 'Em All*, 58, 59.

15. Carlson, "Operations on Makin," 2.

16. Merrill interview.

17. LeFrançois, "We Mopped Up Makin," 23.

18. Peatross, *Bless 'Em All*, 78.

19. Carlson, "Operations on Makin," 3.

20. Nimitz, "Solomon Island Campaign—Makin Island Diversion," 4.

21. Carlson, "Operations on Makin," 4.

22. David W. Haughey, "Carlson's Raid on Makin Island," *American History Illustrated* 18, no. 6 (1983): 62–65.

23. Peatross, *Bless 'Em All*, 60.

24. Ibid., 60, 53.

25. Ibid., 80.

26. Carlson, "Operations on Makin," 4, 5.

27. Peatross, *Bless 'Em All*, 80.

28. Lamb, "Comments on the Raid on Makin Island Manuscript," 11.

29. Peatross, *Bless 'Em All*, 81.

30. Ibid.

31. Lamb, "Comments on the Raid on Makin Island Manuscript," 11.

32. In his "Comments on the Raid on Makin Island Manuscript," Charles Lamb references a copy of the surrender note published in *Dai Toa Senshi* (Story of the Greater East Asia War), vol. 2 (n.p., 1953), 470.

33. Peatross, *Bless 'Em All*, 65.

34. Hoffman, *From Makin to Bougainville*, 8.

35. Benjamin Carson, telephone interview by the author, October 19, 2000.

36. Blankfort, *Big Yankee*, 61.

37. Lamb, "Comments on the Raid on Makin Island Manuscript," 11.

38. General Peatross describes Pfc. Fred Kemp returning to the submarines by paddling with M-1 rifles. Peatross, *Bless 'Em All*, 61.

39. Ibid.

40. Ibid., 65.

41. Ibid., 61.

42. Ibid.

43. Peatross notes that Pvt. Carlyle O. Larson was thought to have volunteered to take a towline to the beach to assist the Raiders. It is possible that Larson, while not a part of the rescue party, was involved in the rescue attempt. He was not seen by any of the Raiders, and they believe he died during the rescue attempt. His body was recovered by the U.S. Army Central Identification Laboratory–Hawaii, in November 1999 in the grave pit on Makin that the Japanese had ordered dug. Peatross, *Bless 'Em All*, 87.

44. Carlson, "Operations on Makin," 5.

45. Ibid.

46. LeFrançois, "We Mopped Up Makin."

47. Carlson, "Operations on Makin," 6. Also referenced in Holmes, *Undersea Victory*, 166. Holmes references the intelligence recovered on Makin: "Some interesting Japanese charts of the Gilbert Islands were recovered, but these turned out on translation to be the Japanese copies of the original American plates that had been given to the Japanese Navy after the Tokyo earthquake."

48. "The boat was straffed and nothing more was seen of it or of the crew. . . . Our own dead on this northern front numbered eleven, including my intelligence officer, Lieutenant Holtom, who had been up on the right flank looking for me. Our other three men killed in action were members of Lieutenant Peatross' boat crew, which landed behind the enemy lines to the south." Carlson's statements on Raiders killed in action and the missing five-man rescue boat crew in Carlson, "Operations on Makin," 6.

49. Peatross, *Bless 'Em All*, 83.

50. McCullough interview.

51. Lamb, "Comments on the Raid on Makin Island Manuscript," 12.

52. Peatross, *Bless 'Em All, 84.*

53. Ibid.

54. Cdr. John M. Haines, "Report of Marine-Submarine Raider Expedition," August 24, 1942, RG 127, Records of the United States Marine Corps, Historical Files, box 183, 370-D-04-1, National Archives, College Park, MD, 6.

55. U.S. Army Central Identification Laboratory, Hawaii, anthropologist Dr. Bill Belcher led a mission to Makin Island in 1999 to recover the Raiders' remains. According to Dr. Belcher, the islanders still refer to the Raiders as the "submarines." Dr. William Belcher, interview by the author, October 19, 2000.

56. In a 1946 AP dispatch referenced in Blankfort's *The Big Yankee* (p. 67), Carlson stated, "If I had knowledge that any Raiders remained on the island at the time we left, I would either have evacuated them or remained with them."

57. Graham, *Mantle of Heroism*, 13.

Chapter 3: Conflicting Reports

1. Lamb, "Comments on the Raid on Makin Island Manuscript," 1.

2. Peatross, *Bless 'Em All*, 86.

3. The raid's results are portrayed as perfect in news articles from the *New York Times*, August 22 and 28, 1942, and in the naval history by Clay Blair Jr., *Silent Victory: The U.S. Submarine War Against Japan* (Philadelphia: J. B. Lippincott, 1975).

4. Carlson, "Operations on Makin," 5.

5. Ibid., 9.

6. Nimitz, "Solomon Island Campaign—Makin Island Diversion," 4.

7. Carson interview, October 19, 2000.

8. Peatross, *Bless 'Em All*, 85.

9. Ibid., 82.

10. It is generally believed that Captain Coyte wrote the surrender note. Ibid.

11. Blankfort, *The Big Yankee*, 60.

12. Carlson, "Operations on Makin," 6.

13. Haines, "Report of Marine-Submarine Raider Expedition."

14. Peatross, *Bless 'Em All*, 86.

15. Carlson comments from an AP dispatch report, May 22, 1946, quoted in Blankfort, *The Big Yankee*, 67.

16. Carlson, "Operations on Makin," 5.

17. "Carlson himself had gone over the battlefield and counted the dead. According to his report, '[o]ur own dead on this northern [northeastern] front numbered eleven, including . . . Lieutenant Holtom. . . . Our other three men killed in action were members of Lieutenant Peatross' [*sic*] boat crew. . . . ' Obviously he, or some of his helpers, miscounted or failed to find some of the bodies, for the final tally of our dead on the 'northern front' alone was 15, including Lieutenant Holtom." Peatross's comments on Carlson's count of Raiders killed in action in *Bless 'Em All*, 86.

18. Carlson, May 22, 1946, AP dispatch report, quoted in Blankfort, *The Big Yankee*, 67.

19. As Raiders returned to the *Nautilus* with news of the ordeal on-shore, Peatross relayed the information to his superiors: "As the senior Marine aboard, it was my duty to keep both Commodore Haines and Captain Brockman informed." Peatross, *Bless 'Em All*, 65.

20. Haines, "Report of Marine-Submarine Raider Expedition," 14.

21. Ibid.

22. Ibid.

23. Ibid.

24. Blankfort, *The Big Yankee*, 38.

25. Nimitz, "Solomon Island Campaign—Makin Island Diversion."

26. Peatross, *Bless 'Em All*, 48.

27. Carson interview, September 21, 2001.

28. Haines, "Report of Marine-Submarine Raider Expedition."

29. Ibid.

30. Adm. R. H. English, "Report of Raider Expedition Against Makin, Comments On," September 3, 1942, RG 127, Records of the United States Marine Corps, Historical Files, box 183, 370-D-04-1, National Archives, College Park, MD.

31. Nimitz, "Solomon Island Campaign—Makin Island Diversion," 6.

32. Ibid.

33. Ibid.

34. Ibid.

35. English, "Report of Raider Expedition Against Makin," 3.

36. Samuel E. Stavisky, *Marine Combat Correspondent: World War II in the Pacific* (New York: Ballantine, 1999), 34.

37. Samuel E. Stavisky, e-mail interview by the author, August 17, 2004.

38. Stavisky, *Marine Combat Correspondent*, 37.

39. Ibid.

Chapter 4: The Left Behind

1. Carlson, "Operations on Makin," 7.

2. Rosenquist, Sexton, and Buerlein, eds., *Our Kind of War*, 57.

3. A. George Noran, "Journal of A. George Noran," Gilbert Islands, January 1943, Marine Corps Historical Center, Washington, DC, 9, 10.

4. Ibid., 13, 16.

5. Ibid., 16.

6. Ibid., 17.

7. Ibid., 19.

8. Peatross, *Bless 'Em All*, 87.

9. Commander Marianas to Headquarters U.S. Army Forces, Middle Pacific, May 13, 1946, Individual Deceased Personnel File of Sgt. Robert V. Allard, National Archives, Suitland, MD.

10. Noran, "Journal of A. George Noran," 20, 21.

11. Benis M. Frank and Henry I. Shaw, *Victory and Occupation: History of U.S. Marine Corps Operations in World War II* (Washington, DC: Historical Branch, U.S. Marine Corps, 1968), 5:745.

12. Noran, "Journal of A. George Noran," 22, 23.

13. Ibid., 23, 24.

14. Donald S. Detwiler and Charles B. Burdicle, *War in Asia and the Pacific, 1937–1949: A Fifteen Volume Collection*, vol. 5, *The Naval Armament Program and Naval Operations* (New York: Garland, 1980), 12. Translated Japanese documents found in *War in Asia* further validate Noran's version of the seizure of Makin: "Japanese Monograph No. 161: Inner South Seas Island Area Naval Operations—Part I: Gilbert Islands Operations." Noran's account of events is very similar to the accounts of the takeover of Betio in Martin Russ, *Line of Departure: Tarawa* (Garden City, NJ: Doubleday, 1975), 1.

15. Detwiler and Burdicle, *War in Asia and the Pacific*, 5:12.

16. *Case of Vice Admiral Koso Abe, IJN; Captain Yoshio Obara, IJN; and Lt. Cdr. Hisakichi Naiki, IJN*, 1948, RG 127, Records of the

United States Marine Corps History and Museum Division Reports, Studies and Plans Relating to World War II Military Operations, 1941–46, box 14, NN3-127-972 (92-0010), National Archives, College Park, MD, 46.

17. Ibid., 53.

18. George Hicks, *The Comfort Women: Japan's Brutal Regime of Enforced Prostitution in the Second World War* (New York: Norton, 1997).

19. Dirk Anthony Ballendorf, *Pete Ellis: An Amphibious Warfare Prophet, 1880–1923* (Annapolis: Naval Institute Press, 1996).

20. Robert D. Heinl and John A. Crown, *The Marshalls: Increasing the Tempo* (Washington, DC: Historical Branch, U.S. Marine Corps, 1954), 86.

21. John Winton, *War in the Pacific: Pearl Harbor to Tokyo Bay* (New York: Mayflower Books, 1978), 106, 107. See also William A. Renzi and Mark D. Roehrs, *Never Look Back: A History of World War II in the Pacific* (New York: M. E. Sharpe, 1991), 96.

22. Peatross, *Bless 'Em All*, 87.

23. Ray Bauml, "K.I.A.: The Eighteen Marines Killed in Action During the 17–18 August 1942 Raid on Makin Island," *1994 Raider Patch*, 107.

24. Carson interview, October 19, 2000.

25. Ray Bauml, "M.I.A.: The Twelve Enlisted Marines Listed as Missing in Action Against the Enemy on the Raid on Makin Island," *1994 Raider Patch*, 106.

26. *Riddles of the Dead: Execution Island*, VHS, directed and produced by James M. Felter (Takoma Park, MD: Hoggard Film Productions, 2002).

27. William P. Mahoney, "Son of an Immigrant" (unpublished memoir, in the author's possession), 95. In support of naval war crimes investigations in the Pacific, Mahoney visited Makin Island. He recounts his visit in this unpublished memoir.

28. Of the eleven Raiders who could conceivably be the nine missing

Raiders, eight are listed as Protestants, two are listed as "no reli-gious preference," and only one is listed as Catholic. Individual Deceased Personnel Files of Cpl. James Beecher, Pvt. Cletus Smith, Sgt. Robert V. Allard, Sgt. Dallas H. Cook, Cpl. James Gifford, Pfc. Richard E. Davis, Pfc. Richard N. Olbert, Pfc. William E. Pallesen, Pvt. John I. Kerns, Pvt. Alden C. Mattison, Pvt. Donald R. Roberton, National Archives, Suitland, MD.

29. Mahoney, "Son of an Immigrant," 95.

30. Sei'ichiro Tamura, letter to Hitoshi Kawano, May 23, 2001. Copy provided to the author on August 26, 2001. Hitoshi Kawano, in attempt to learn more about the Raiders' fate, requested informa-tion from Japanese veterans in a Japanese veterans newsletter. Mr. Tamura responded with information concerning the Raiders' transport to Kwajalein.

Chapter 5: Victors' Justice

1. Yoshio Obara, "Statement of Obara, Yoshio, Formerly Captain, Imperial Japanese Navy, Pertaining to Execution of American Pris-oners on Kwajalein October 1942," March 13, 1946, RG 127, Records of the United States Marine Corps History and Museum Division Reports, Studies and Plans Relating to World War II Military Ops, 1941–46, box 14, NN3-127-972 (92—0010), Ex-hibit 3B, National Archives, College Park, MD.

2. Eugene Soviak, *The Wartime Diary of Kiyosawa Kiyoshi*, trans. Marius Jansen and Kamiyama Tamie (Princeton: Princeton Uni-versity Press, 1999), 92. A direct result of this prevalent attitude of the Japanese toward POWs is addressed in Yuki Tanaka, *Hid-den Horrors: Japanese War Crimes in World War II* (Boulder, CO: Westview Press, 1998). Tanaka describes poison, starvation, and malaria experiments that were conducted by the Japanese on POWs in the southwest Pacific. Gavan Daws also addresses the mistreatment of Allied POWs in the Pacific in his *Prisoners of*

the Japanese: POWs of World War II in the Pacific (New York: W. Morrow, 1994).

3. "In November 1943 when Makin Atoll was recaptured by our forces, Major Roosevelt accompanied the landing force specifically to attempt to determine the fate of the missing Raiders. After interviewing all available witnesses, he established that a common grave on Butaritari was the final resting place of 18 Raiders, and nine had been imprisoned by the Japanese, thus leaving three unaccounted for." Peatross, *Bless 'Em All*, 87.

4. Lamb, "Comments on the Raid on Makin Island Manuscript." Additionally, in an interview with the author, Raider Kenneth H. Merrill commented that he believed he first heard of the left-behind Raiders' execution from a Tokyo Rose broadcast during the war.

5. *Final Report of Navy War Crimes Program.*

6. Nathan G. Finkelstein, "Record of Proceedings of War Crimes Investigations Conducted at Maloelap and Majuro Atolls, Marshall Islands," October 13, 1945–November 29, 1945, RG 125, Navy JAG Records, box 12, NN3-125-91-001, National Archives, College Park, MD.

7. Adm. George Murray, letter to Capt. John D. Murphy, March 12, 1946, Papers of Admiral John D. Murphy, 1943–1949, Hoover Institution, Stanford, CA.

8. Headquarters American Graves Registration Service (Pacific Zone) APO 958, "Proceedings of Board of Review," January 3, 1950, Individual Deceased Personnel File of 2nd Lt. Virgil A. Tramelli, National Archives, Suitland, MD.

9. Murray letter.

10. Edwin P. Hoyt, *To the Marianas: War in the Central Pacific, 1944* (New York: Van Nostrand Reinhold, 1980), 21.

11. Mahoney, "Son of an Immigrant," 93.

12. In his unpublished memoir, Mahoney describes the meeting with Abe as taking place at the prison; however, trial testimony places

the interrogation at the Forty-second General Hospital in Tokyo, Japan. Mahoney, "Son of an Immigrant," 93. See also *Case of Vice Admiral Koso Abe*.

13. Coincidentally the Japanese language officer of the Raiders, Gerald P. Holtom, who was killed during the raid, was, as was Osborne, a graduate of the Japanese Language School at Boulder.

14. Lejana Lekot, "Statement of Lejana, Marshallese Native," December 12, 1945, RG 125, Navy JAG Records, box 8, NN3 125-91 009, National Archives, College Park, MD.

15. Mahoney, "Son of an Immigrant," 94.

16. "Interrogation of Abe, Koso, Formerly Vice Admiral, Imperial Japanese Navy, by Commander Murphy and Lieutenant Mahoney, Tokyo, Japan," March 2, 1946, RG 127, Records of the United States Marine Corps History and Museum Division Reports, Studies and Plans Relating to World War II Military Ops, 1941–46, Box 14, NN3-127-972 (92-0010), National Archives, College Park, MD.

17. "Interrogation of Abe."

18. Mahoney, "Son of an Immigrant," 95.

19. Ibid.

20. Obara, "Statement of Obara."

21. Ibid.

22. Ibid.

23. Edward L. Field, telephone interview by the author, May 25, 2001.

24. "Opening Statement of Koso Abe Trial Presented by Lt. Edward L. Field," in *Case of Vice Admiral Koso Abe*.

25. *Case of Vice Admiral Koso Abe*, 4–7.

26. Ibid., 52.

27. Ibid., 76.

28. Frank and Shaw, *Victory and Occupation*, 5:745.

29. Hisakichi Naiki, "Basic Personnel Record: Alien Enemy or Prisoner of War," RG 554, Sugamo Prison Records, box 99, 290-66-231, National Archives, College Park, MD. See also Yoshio Obara,

"Basic Personnel Record: Alien Enemy or Prisoner of War," RG 554, Sugamo Prison Records, box 99, 290-66-231, National Archives, College Park, MD.

30. *Final Report of Navy War Crimes Program.*

Chapter 6: Pacific Heroes

1. *Nihango: Japanese Language*, s.v. "kantai," http://www.trussel.com/f_nih.ht (accessed October 11, 2001).

2. Marine Corps historians Benis M. Frank and Henry I. Shaw accepted the Japanese officers' war crimes testimony concerning Japanese treatment of POWs on Kwajalein as fact in *Victory and Occupation*, 745.

3. *Case of Vice Admiral Koso Abe*, 60.

4. Headquarters American Graves Registration Service, "Non-Recoverability of Remains Memorandum to Board of Review."

5. Capt. Louis Silvie Zamperini, "Testimony of Captain Zamperini to Special Agent Ralph W. Montgomery, Counter Intelligence Corps, Sixth Army," in the author's possession.

6. Louis Zamperini, telephone interview by the author, April 16, 2001.

7. *Case of Vice Admiral Koso Abe*, 7.

8. Nixon Braind, interview by the author, February 15, 2002.

9. Capt. Russell Allen Phillips, "Affidavit to Commander M. E. Currie, January 11, 1948," Papers of Admiral John D. Murphy, 1943–1949, Hoover Institution, Stanford, CA.

10. "Among the human guinea pigs were an undetermined number of American soldiers, captured during the early part of the war and confined in prisoner of war camps in Manchuria." John W. Powell Jr., "Japan's Biological Weapons: 1930–1945, a Hidden Chapter in History," *Bulletin of Atomic Scientists*, October 1981, quoted in Sheldon H. Harris, *Factories of Death: Japanese Biological Warfare, 1932–45, and the American Cover-Up* (New York: Routledge, 1994), 116.

11. Zamperini, "Testimony of Captain Zamperini."

12. Capt. Fred F. Garrett, "Affidavit to M. E. Currie, Commander U.S. Naval Reserve," January 7, 1948, Papers of Adm. John D. Murphy, 1943–1949, Hoover Institution, Stanford, CA.

13. According to Mr. Anni Betwel, a Marshall Islander, a week before the 1944 U.S. invasion he and his family witnessed Japanese soldiers executing two "U.S. Navy pilots." It is possible that these "pilots" were the POWs Tinker described. Anni Betwel, interview by the author, February 13, 2002.

14. Garrett, "Affidavit to M. E. Currie," 2.

Chapter 7: Carlson and Roosevelt After the Raid

1. Hoffman, *From Makin to Bougainville*, 25.

2. Ibid., 3.

3. Ibid., 25.

4. Dr. Charles M. Grossman, telephone interview by the author, April 14, 2003.

5. Janet Stevenson, *The Undiminished Man: A Political Biography of Robert Walker Kenny* (Novato, CA: Chandler and Sharp, 1980), 58.

6. Roosevelt interview, 1.

7. Ibid. See also "Roosevelt, James, 1907–1991," *Biographical Directory of the United States Congress, 1774–Present*, http:// bioguide.congress.gov/scripts/biodisplay.pl?index=R000426 (accessed on September 3, 2003).

Chapter 8: The Search for the Forgotten Raiders

1. U.S. Army Central Identification Laboratory, Hawaii (undated pamphlet).

2. *Defense Prisoner of War/Missing Personnel Office*, http:// www.dtic.mil/dpmo/ (accessed on August 11, 2005).

Chapter 9: A Search Through History

1. On our first mission to Kwajalein, archeologist Greg Fox and I

carried the remains of this individual to the Marshall Islands for repatriation in Kiribati (Makin).

2. Lt. Col. Gilbert Wong, "Summary of Pertinent Facts on Case No. 308," Individual Deceased Personnel File of 2nd Lt. Virgil A. Tramelli, National Archives, Suitland, MD.

3. Ibid.

Chapter 11: Good News

1. The author shared his original thesis and research with representatives of Hoggard Film Company who collaborated with National Geographic and produced the *Riddles of the Dead: Execution Island* documentary. It has aired in the United Kingdom since 2002.

2. *Case of Vice Admiral Koso Abe*, 53.

3. The USS *Makin Island* (LHD-8) is not the first Navy vessel to be named for the Makin raid. The USS *Makin Island* (CVE-93), a Casablanca-class escort carrier, was commissioned in 1944, saw combat in the Pacific in World War II, and was scrapped in 1947.

4. *USS* Makin Island*, LHD-8*, http://www.makin-island.navy.mil (accessed August 12, 2006).

BIBLIOGRAPHY

Unpublished Manuscript Collections

Abe, Koso. "Basic Personnel Record: Alien Enemy or Prisoner of War." RG 554, Sugamo Prison Records, box 99, 290-66-231, National Archives, College Park, MD.

Carlson, Lt. Col. Evans F. "Operations on Makin, August 17–18, 1942, Written Onboard USS *Nautilus*, at Sea." August 21, 1942. RG 127, Records of the United States Marine Corps, Historical Files, box 183, 370-D-04-1, National Archives, College Park, MD.

Case of Vice Admiral Koso Abe, IJN; Captain Yoshio Obara, IJN; and Lt. Cdr. Hisakichi Naiki, IJN. 1948. RG 127, Records of the United States Marine Corps History and Museum Division Reports, Studies and Plans Relating to World War II Military Operations, 1941–46, box 14, NN3-127-972 (92-0010), National Archives, College Park, MD.

Commander Marianas, letter to Headquarters U.S. Army Forces, Middle Pacific, May 13, 1946. Individual Deceased Personnel File of Sgt. Robert V. Allard. National Archives, Suitland, MD.

English, Adm. R. H. "Report of Raider Expedition Against Makin, Comments on." September 3, 1942. RG 127, Records of the United States Marine Corps, Historical Files, box 183, 370-D-04-1, National Archives, College Park, MD.

Final Report of Navy War Crimes Program Submitted by the Director, War Crimes, U.S. Pacific Fleet to the Secretary of the Navy. December 1, 1949. Microfilm, NRS1977-57, Navy Historical Center, Washington, DC.

Finkelstein, Nathan G. "Record of Proceedings of War Crimes Investigations Conducted at Maloelap and Majuro Atolls, Marshall Islands." October 13, 1945–November 29, 1945. RG 125, Navy JAG Records, box 12, NN3-125-91-001, National Archives, College Park, MD.

Garrett, Capt. Fred F. "Affidavit to M. E. Currie, Commander U.S. Naval Reserve." January 7, 1948. Papers of Adm. John D. Murphy, 1943–1949. Hoover Institution, Stanford, CA.

Haines, Cdr. John M. "Report of Marine-Submarine Raider Expedition." August 24, 1942. RG 127, Records of the United States Marine Corps, Historical Files, box 183, 370-D-04-1, National Archives, College Park, MD.

Headquarters American Graves Registration Service (Pacific Zone) APO 958. "Proceedings of Board of Review," January 3, 1950. Individual Deceased Personnel File of 2nd Lt. Virgil A. Tramelli. National Archives, Suitland, MD.

Individual Deceased Personnel Files of Cpl. James Beecher, Pvt. Cletus Smith, Sgt. Robert V. Allard, Sgt. Dallas H. Cook, Cpl. James Gifford, Pfc. Richard E. Davis, Pfc. Richard N. Olbert, Pfc. William E. Pallesen, Pvt. John I. Kerns, Pvt. Alden C. Mattison, Pvt. Donald R. Roberton. National Archives, Suitland, MD.

"Interrogation of Abe, Koso, formerly Vice Admiral, Imperial Japanese Navy, by Commander Murphy and Lieutenant

Mahoney, Tokyo, Japan." March 2, 1946. RG 127, Records of the United States Marine Corps History and Museum Division Reports, Studies and Plans Relating to World War II Military OPS, 1941–46, box 14, NN3-127-972 (92-0010), National Archives, College Park, MD.

Lamb, Charles. "Comments on the Raid on Makin Island Manuscript," Lamb Papers, Marine Corps Research Center, Quantico, VA.

Lekot, Lejana. "Statement of Lejana, Marshallese Native." December 12, 1945. RG 125, Navy JAG Records, box 8, NN3 125-91 009, National Archives, College Park, MD.

Mahoney, William P. "Son of an Immigrant." Unpublished memoir. In the author's possession.

Marine Raider Association. "The Raid at Makin Island." James Roosevelt Papers, box 761957-58. Franklin D. Roosevelt Library, Hyde Park, NY.

Murray, Adm. George D., letter to Capt. John D. Murphy, March 12, 1946. Papers of Adm. John D. Murphy, 1943–1949. Hoover Institution, Stanford, CA.

Naiki, Hisakichi. "Basic Personnel Record: Alien Enemy or Prisoner of War." RG 554, Sugamo Prison Records, box 99, 290-66-231, National Archives, College Park, MD.

Nimitz, Adm. Chester. "Solomon Island Campaign—Makin Island Diversion." October 20, 1942. RG 127, Records of the United States Marine Corps, Historical Files, box 183, 370-D-04-1, National Archives, College Park, MD.

Noran, A. George. "Journal of A. George Noran." Gilbert Islands. January 1943. Marine Corps Historical Center, Washington, DC.

Obara, Yoshio. "Basic Personnel Record: Alien Enemy or Prisoner of War." RG 554, Sugamo Prison Records, box 99, 290-66-231, National Archives, College Park, MD.

————. "Statement of Obara, Yoshio, Formerly Captain, Imperial Japanese Navy, Pertaining to Execution of American Prisoners on Kwajalein October 1942." March 13, 1946. RG 127, Records of the United States Marine Corps History and Museum Division Reports, Studies and Plans Relating to World War II Military OPS, 1941–46, box 14, NN3-127-972 (92-0010), Exhibit 3B, National Archives, College Park, MD.

Phillips, Capt. Russell Allen. "Affidavit to Commander M. E. Currie, January 11, 1948." Papers of Adm. John D. Murphy, 1943–1949. Hoover Institution, Stanford, CA.

Tamura, Sei'ichiro, letter to Hitoshi Kawano. May 23, 2001. In author's possession.

Thacker, Joel D. "The Marine Raiders in World War II (Preliminary)." Historical Branch Assistant Chief of Staff, G-3 Headquarters, U.S. Marine Corps, 1954.

Wong, Lt. Col. Gilbert. "Summary of Pertinent Facts on Case No. 308." Individual Deceased Personnel File of 2nd Lt. Virgil A. Tramelli. National Archives, Suitland, MD.

Zamperini, Capt. Louis Silvie. "Affidavit to Captain Robert M. Musick, November 1, 1945." Papers of Adm. John D. Murphy, 1943–1949. Hoover Institution, Stanford, CA.

————. "Testimony of Captain Zamperini to Special Agent Ralph W. Montgomery, Counter Intelligence Corps–Sixth Army." In the author's possession.

Zimmerman, Phyllis. "The First 'Gung Ho' Marine: Evans F. Carlson of the Raiders." Unpublished manuscript. 1999. In the author's possession.

Published Primary Sources

Carlson, Evans Fordyce. *The Chinese Army: Its Organization and Military Efficiency*. New York: International Secretariat, Institute of Pacific Relations, 1940.

———. *Evans F. Carlson on China at War, 1937–1941*. Edited by Hugh Deane. New York: China and U.S. Publication, 1993.

———. *Twin Stars of China: A Behind the Scenes Story of China's Valiant Struggle for Existence, by a U.S. Marine Who Lived and Moved with the People*. New York: Dodd, Mead, 1940.

Detwiler, Donald S., and Charles B. Burdick, eds. *War in Asia and the Pacific, 1937–1949: A Fifteen Volume Collection*. Vol. 5, *The Naval Armament Program and Naval Operations*. New York: Garland, 1980.

Goldstein, Donald M., and Katherine V. Dillon. *Fading Victory: The Diary of Admiral Matome Ogaki, 1941–1945*. Translated by Masataka Chihaya. Pittsburgh: University of Pittsburgh Press, 1991.

Military Intelligence Service Veterans Club of Hawaii. *Secret Valor: M.I.S. Personnel, World War II, Pacific Theater, Pre-Pearl Harbor to Sept 8, 1951*. Honolulu: Military Intelligence Service Veterans, 1993.

Peatross, Maj. Gen. Oscar F. *Bless 'Em All: The Marine Raiders of World War II*. Irvine, CA: ReView Publications, 1995.

Roster of Graduates. Japanese Language School Archives. University of Colorado at Boulder Libraries.

South Suburban Chicago Detachment #663, *Marine Corps League RESOLUTION*. Passed at National Convention at New Orleans, LA, August 17, 2000. (Resolution to request that the Senate subcommittee on POW/MIA affairs identify, recover, and return to the families the remains of the nine Raiders who were beheaded and secure an apology from the Japanese government to the next of kin.)

Zamperini, Louis. *Devil at My Heels: The Story of Louis Zamperini*. Edited by Helen Itris. London: Peter Davies, 1956.

Secondary Sources

Alexander, Joseph D. *Storm Landings: Epic Amphibious Battles in the Central Pacific*. Annapolis: Naval Institute Press, 1997.

―――. *Utmost Savagery: The Three Days of Tarawa*. New York: Ivy Books, 1995.

Ballendorf, Dirk Anthony. *Pete Ellis: An Amphibious Warfare Prophet, 1880–1923*. Annapolis: Naval Institute Press, 1996.

Bartlett, Merrill L. *Assault From the Sea: Essays on the History of Amphibious Warfare*. Annapolis: Naval Institute Press, 1983.

Blankfort, Michael. *The Big Yankee: The Life of Carlson of the Raiders*. Boston: Little, Brown, 1947.

Blair, Clay, Jr. *Silent Victory: The U.S. Submarine War Against Japan*. Philadelphia: J. B. Lippincott, 1975.

Carter, Kit C., and Robert Mueller. *The Army Air Forces in World War II: Combat Chronology, 1941–1945*. Washington, DC: U.S. Government Printing Office, 1973.

Cope, Harley, and Walter Karig. *Battle Submerged: Submarine Fighters of World War II*. New York: Norton, 1951.

Craven, W. F., and J. L. Cate, eds. *The Army Air Forces in World War II*. Vol. 4, *The Pacific: Guadalcanal to Saipan, August 1942 to July 1944*. Washington, DC: U.S. Government Printing Office, 1983.

Daws, Gavan. *Prisoners of the Japanese: POWS of World War II in the Pacific*. New York: W. Morrow, 1994.

Dower, John W. *War Without Mercy: Race and Power in the Pacific*. New York: Pantheon Books, 1986.

Dull, Paul S. *A Battle History of the Imperial Japanese Navy, 1941–1945*. Annapolis: Naval Institute Press, 1978.

―――. *The Tokyo Trials: A Functional Index to the Proceedings of the International Military Tribunal for the Far East*. Ann Arbor: Michigan University Press, 1957.

Eller, Ernest M. *United States Submarine Losses: World War II*. Washington, DC: U.S. Government Printing Office, 1950.

Frank, Benis M., and Henry I. Shaw. *Victory and Occupation: History of U.S. Marine Corps Operations in World War II*. Vol. 5. Washington, DC: Historical Branch, U.S. Marine Corps, 1968.

Garrett, Richard. *The Raiders: The Elite Strike Forces That Altered the Course of War and History*. New York: Van Nostrand Reinhold, 1980.

Graham, Michael B. *Mantle of Heroism: Tarawa and the Struggle for the Gilberts, November 1943*. Novato, CA: Presidio Press, 1993.

Harris, Sheldon H. *Factories of Death: Japanese Biological Warfare, 1932–45, and the American Cover-Up*. New York: Routledge, 1994.

Heinl, Robert Debs. *Soldiers of the Sea: The United States Marine Corps, 1775–1962*. Annapolis: U.S. Naval Institute, 1962.

Heinl, Robert D., and John A. Crown. *The Marshalls: Increasing the Tempo*. Washington, DC: Historical Branch, U.S. Marine Corps, 1954.

Hicks, George. *The Comfort Women: Japan's Brutal Regime of Enforced Prostitution in the Second World War*. New York: Norton, 1997.

Hinz, Earl. *Pacific Island Battlegrounds of World War II: Then and Now*. Honolulu: Bess Press, 1995.

Hoffman, Maj. Jon T. *From Makin to Bougainville: Marine Raiders in the Pacific War*. Washington, DC: Marine Corps Historical Center, 1995.

Holmes, W. J. *Undersea Victory: The Influence of Submarine Operations on the War in the Pacific*. Garden City, NY: Doubleday, 1966.

Hough, Frank O., Verle Ludwig, and Henry I. Shaw Jr., eds. *History of U.S. Marine Corps Operations in World War II.* Vol. 1, *Pearl Harbor to Guadalcanal.* Washington, DC: U.S. Government Printing Office, 1958.

Hoyt, Edwin P. *To the Marianas: War in the Central Pacific, 1944.* New York: Van Nostrand Reinhold, 1980.

Levine, Alan J. *The Pacific War: Japan Versus the Allies.* London: Praeger, 1995.

Maga, Timothy. *Judgment at Tokyo: The Japanese War Crimes Trials.* Lexington: University Press of Kentucky, 2001.

Marshall, S. L. A. *Island Victory: The Battle for Kwajalein Atoll.* Washington, DC: Infantry Journal, 1945.

Millett, Allan Reed. *Semper Fidelis: The History of the United States Marine Corps.* New York: Macmillan, 1980.

Morison, Samuel Eliot. *History of United States Naval Operations in World War II.* Vol. 4, *Coral Sea, Midway and Submarine Actions, May 1942–August 1942.* Boston: Little, Brown, 1949.

―――. *The Two Ocean War: A Short History of the United States Navy in the Second World War.* Boston: Little, Brown, 1963.

Moskin, Robert J. *The U.S. Marine Corps Story.* New York: McGraw Hill, 1982.

Potter, E. B. *Nimitz.* Annapolis: Naval Institute Press, 1976.

Prados, John. *Combined Fleet Decoded: The Secret History of American Intelligence and the Japanese Navy in World War II.* New York: Random House, 1995.

Rath, J. Arthur. *Soldiers Remember: World War II in the Pacific.* Syracuse, NY: J. Arthur Rath, 1995.

Renzi, William A., and Mark D. Roehrs. *Never Look Back: A History of World War II in the Pacific.* New York: M. E. Sharpe, 1991.

Roscoe, Theodore. *United States Submarine Operations in World War II.* Annapolis: U.S. Naval Institute, 1949.

Rosenquist, R. G., Col. Martin J. "Stormy" Sexton, USMC (Ret.), and Robert A. Buerlein, eds. *Our Kind of War: Illustrated Saga of the U.S. Marine Raiders of World War II*. Richmond, VA: American Historical Foundation, 1990.

Russ, Martin. *Line of Departure: Tarawa*. Garden City, NY: Doubleday, 1975.

Shaw, Henry I., Jr., Bernard C. Nalty, and Edwin T. Turnbladh, eds. *Central Pacific Drive: History of U.S. Marine Corps Operations in World War II*. Vol. 3. Washington, DC: U.S. Government Printing Office, 1966.

Simmons, Edwin H. *The United States Marines, 1775–1975*. New York: Viking Press, 1976.

Soviak, Eugene. *The Wartime Diary of Kiyosawa Kiyoshi*. Translated by Marius Jansen and Kamiyama Tamie. Princeton: Princeton University Press, 1999.

Spector, Ronald H. *Eagle Against the Sun: The American War With Japan*. New York: Free Press, 1985.

———. *Listening to the Enemy: Key Documents on the Role of Communications and Intelligence in the War with Japan*. Wilmington: Scholarly Resources, 1988.

Spennemann, Dirk H. R. *The Last Flight of the "St Quentin Quail": Investigations of the Wreckage and History of Consolidated B-24D "Liberator" Aircraft #42-41205 off Jab'u Island, Arno Atoll, Republic of the Marshall Islands*. Albury: Charles Sturt University, 1994.

Stavisky, Samuel E. *Marine Combat Correspondent: World War II in the Pacific*. New York: Ballantine, 1999.

Stevenson, Janet. *The Undiminished Man: A Political Biography of Robert Walker Kenny*. Novato, CA: Chandler and Sharp, 1980.

Tanaka, Yuki. *Hidden Horrors: Japanese War Crimes in World War II*. Boulder, CO: Westview Press, 1998.

Updegraph, Charles L. *U.S. Marine Corps Special Units of World War II.* Washington, DC: History and Museums Division, 1977.

Wells, Mark K. *Courage and Air Warfare: The Allied Aircrew Experience in the Second World War.* Portland: Frank Cass, 1997.

Wheeler, Keith. *War Under the Pacific.* Chicago: Time Life Books, 1980.

Wheeler, Richard. *A Special Valor: The U.S. Marines and the Pacific War.* New York: Harper & Row, 1983.

Winton, John. *War in the Pacific: Pearl Harbor to Tokyo Bay.* New York: Mayflower Books, 1978.

Periodicals

Bauml, Ray. "K.I.A.: The Eighteen Marines Killed in Action During the 17–18 August 1942 Raid on Makin Island." *1994 Raider Patch.*

———. "M.I.A.: The Twelve Enlisted Marines Listed as Missing in Action Against the Enemy on the Raid on Makin Island." *1994 Raider Patch.*

Haughey, David W. "Carlson's Raid on Makin Island." *American History Illustrated* 18, no. 6 (1983): 62–65.

Kwajalein Veterans of Foreign Wars Post 10268, *The Battles of Kwajalein and Roi-Namur.* N.p.: Bell Telephone Co., 1974.

LeFrançois, Lt. W. S. "We Mopped Up Makin." *Saturday Evening Post,* December 11, 1943, 28–48.

New York Times, August 22 and 28, 1942.

Twining, Merrill B. "An Unhandsome Quitting." *Proceedings* 118, no. 11 (1992): 83–87.

Pamphlet

U.S. Army Central Identification Laboratory, Hawaii (undated pamphlet).

Video Documentary

Riddles of the Dead: Execution Island. VHS. Directed and produced by James M. Felter. Takoma Park, MD: Hoggard Film Productions, 2002.

Websites

Defense Prisoner of War/Missing Personnel Office. http://www.dtic.mil/dpmo/. Accessed August 12, 2005.

Nihango: Japanese Language. s.v. "kantai." http://www.trussel.com/f_nih.ht. Accessed October 11, 2001.

Ozeki, Shigeyoshi. "Wake Island by Sight." Translated by Daniel King. http://astro.temple.edu/~gurwin//foozeki.htm. Accessed August 9, 2005.

"Roosevelt, James, 1907–1991." *Biographical Directory of the United States Congress, 1774–Present.* http://bioguide.congress.gov/scripts/biodisplay.pl?index=R000426. Accessed September 3, 2002.

USS Makin Island, *LHD 8.* http://www.makin-island.navy.mil. Accessed August 12, 2006.

Fiction

Griffin, W. E. B. *The Corps.* Book 2, *Call to Arms.* New York: Jove Books, 1987.

Ludwig, Verle E. *Archie Smallwood and the Marine Raiders.* Santa Barbara, CA: Daniel and Daniel, 1998.

Interviews

Belcher, Dr. William. Interview by the author, October 19, 2000.

Betwel, Anni. Interview by the author, February 13, 2002.

Braind, Nixon. Interview by the author, February 15, 2002.

Carson, Benjamin. Interview by Mr. Graham, September 21, 2001. Transcript. Admiral Nimitz National Museum of the Pacific War, Fredricksburg, TX.

————. Telephone interview by the author, October 19, 2000.

Field, Edward L. Telephone interview by the author, May 25, 2001.

Fukuhara, Col. Harry. Interview by the author, July 24, 2001.

Grossman, Dr. Charles M. Telephone interview by the author, April 14, 2003.

Hudman, Denton E. Telephone interview by the author, March 17, 2003.

Kanel, Menke. Interview by the author, February 13, 2002.

McCullough, Kenneth. Telephone interview by the author, October 25, 2000.

Merrill, Kenneth. Telephone interview by the author, August 13, 2005.

Okubo, Don. Interview by the author, May 7, 2001.

Osborne, Mrs. David. Telephone interview by the author, October 19, 2000.

Roosevelt, James. Interview by Amelia R. Fry, August 10, 1972. In Amelia R. Fry. *California Democrats in the Earl Warren Era : Interviews*. Sanford, NC: Microfilming Corp of America, 1982.

Stavisky, Samuel E. E-mail interview by the author, August 17, 2004.

Tinker, Frank. Telephone interview by the author, April 17, 2001.

Zamperini, Louis. Telephone interview by the author, April 16, 2001.

INDEX

ABOUT THE AUTHOR

TRIPP WILES is a 1995 graduate of The Citadel and a former Army officer. He holds a master's degree in diplomacy and military studies from Hawaii Pacific University, and he worked four years as an analyst at both the Central Identification Laboratory in Hawaii and the Defense Prisoners of War/Missing Personnel Office in Virginia. Tripp and his wife, Lindsay, live in Memphis, Tennessee, where he is a law student at the University of Memphis.